# WordPerfect 6.0 for Windows
# Slick Tricks

# WordPerfect 6.0 for Windows
# Slick Tricks
· · · · · · · · · · · · · · ·

## Kay Yarborough Nelson

**RANDOM HOUSE**
**ELECTRONIC PUBLISHING**

New York

Word Perfect 6.0 for Windows Slick Tricks

Copyright © 1994 by Kay Yarborough Nelson

Produced and composed by Parker-Fields Typesetters, Ltd.

Published in the United States by Random House, Inc., New York, and simultaneously in Canada by Random House of Canada, Limited.

Manufactured in the United States of America

First Edition

0   9   8   7   6   5   4   3   2   1

ISBN  0-679-79165-5

**Trademarks**

New York        Toronto        London        Sydney        Auckland

# Contents

· · · · · · · · · · · · · · · · · · · · · · ·

# Acknowledgments

Many thanks to all who made this book possible: Tracy Smith, Senior Editor at Random House, and Michael Aquilante, Project Editor. These truly professional editors got the job done right, and on time, and it is a pleasure working with them.

Many thanks also to "Uncle" Gus Hallgren, for keeping me supplied with many tips, tricks, and his inexhaustible store of opinions about WordPerfect. Several of the tricks in this book come straight to you from Uncle Gus, user par excellence.

# Introduction

This *Slick Tricks* series is based on a simple idea: You don't have to know a lot about a program to get some real power from it! All of the software you buy today is incredibly rich in features, but most of us will use only a few of them because we don't want to wade through the manual or spend hours working through exercises.

But beyond the programs' intimidating interfaces lies a wealth of tricks that you can master easily—without taking a complex tutorial on a program's whole feature set, or thumbing through a huge doorstop-sized tome. You can flip through the pages of this *Slick Tricks* book, find a topic that's related to what you're working on, and see how to do a trick or use a shortcut that will make your work a lot easier.

## Why Slick Tricks?

Most of these tricks are just that: tricks, short statements about how to use a keyboard shortcut to do something faster, or how to go through a back door to get a complicated sequence done quickly. We're not starting from ground zero and teaching you the program's basics, though. To get the most from a *Slick Tricks* book, you'll at least need to be familiar with the program's absolute basics, such as selecting with a mouse (if you're in a Windows or Macintosh book) or reading a prompt (if you're in a DOS book).

## Using a *Slick Tricks* Book

You can think of a *Slick Tricks* book as a cookbook—browse its pages and try out a "recipe" or two. But these are fairly "right-brained" books, so you may need to browse until you find the recipe you need.

These books offer basic tricks—the ones you'll use all the time—and include tricks for customizing, printing, managing your documents, and any special features of the programs. These short, friendly books can't possibly cover *all* the features of a program or system, but neither would you want them to.

**Trick**

**Tip**

**Trap**

**Sidebar**

You'll see different icons in a *Slick Tricks* book. The professor indicates a hands-on procedure or trick, showing you how to do something. A "Tip" gives you a helpful, general hint about how to approach a task or work out a solution to your problem. "Traps" tell you procedures to avoid, and "sidebars" provide background material for a particular topic. These *Slick Tricks* books won't always take you step by step through every possibility and every detail, but programs today have incredibly good Help systems, and you can use them to get details about a specific topic. So, do that.

Each *Slick Tricks* book follows the general conventions of the program or system it's about. You'll find the keys you need to press in boldface type and what you actually need to type in sans serif type, like this: Press **F12** and type **weekly report**. In all of these, if you need to press two keys at once, you'll see them with a plus sign between them, like this: Press **Ctrl+Z**.

# You're on Your Way

That's it! You can figure out the rest as you go along. For example, if you see any instructions that talk about screen color, just ignore them if you have a monochrome monitor. You may see tips and tricks repeated in different chapters, but that's to keep you from jumping back and forth in the book. Have fun with these books and amaze your friends with what you can do!

# WordPerfect 6.0 for Windows
# Slick Tricks

# Chapter 1

· · · · · · · · · · · · · · · · · · · · · · · · · · · · ·

## Basic Slick Tricks

Aᴸᴛʜᴏᴜɢʜ ᴛʜᴇ ᴛʀɪᴄᴋs ɪɴ ᴛʜɪs ᴄʜᴀᴘᴛᴇʀ ᴀʀᴇ sɪᴍᴘʟᴇ, don't be fooled: Simple tricks—the ones you use for things you do every day—are the real timesavers and keys to productivity. After all, a few keystrokes multiplied over hundreds of times are a lot of keystrokes. These easy slick tricks add up in time you can spend thinking about other work or even being away from the computer.

## What You're Looking At
· · · · · · · · · · · · · · · · · · · · · · · · · · · · ·

WordPerfect has three different modes, or views, and each one is best for some things but not for others.

### Use Draft Mode for Your Input
WordPerfect has three modes—Draft, Page, and Two-Page mode. Draft mode is by far the fastest for inputting raw text. Type your documents in Draft mode; then use Page mode or Two-Page mode to format them.

1

### Switching Back to Draft Mode Quickly

To switch from one view to another, use these quick keyboard short-cuts:

+ **Alt+F5** switches you to Page mode.
+ **Ctrl+F5** switches you back to Draft mode.

### Use Page and Draft Mode for Different Things

Page mode displays pages as they'll actually be printed, complete with headers and footers, font changes, page numbers, notes, watermarks, and top and bottom margins. You don't get a Print Preview screen in WordPerfect 6.0 for Windows because Page and Two-Page modes show it all.

Draft mode displays all font changes and graphic images, but it *doesn't* display headers and footers, page numbers, watermarks, or top and bottom margins.

So the bottom line is: Use Page mode for editing things that aren't displayed in Draft mode. Page and Two-Page modes are both slower than Draft mode. But if you have a very fast computer, you may find that you can use Page mode all the time.

### Customizing Your Screen Display

You can pick which elements you want to display on the screen or use a handy shortcut to hide all the bars at once.

You don't have to display everything that Figure 1.1 is showing, such as the ruler, the button bar, the power bar, the scroll bars, and so forth. For a clean, uncluttered screen, you can turn off most of those displays. To hide everything at once and get a truly clean screen, just press **Alt+Shift+F5**. To get the bars back again once you've turned them off, press **Esc**.

You can also customize most of the menus and bars. Chapter 4, "Tricks for Customizing WordPerfect 6.0," shows you in detail how to set up the editing screen the way you want it. Here are some quick slick tricks to hold you until Chapter 4.

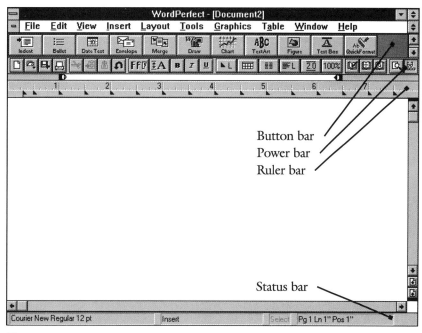

**Figure 1.1**  **Displaying WordPerfect's bars**

### *What Are All Those Buttons For?*

The array of buttons on the button bars can be pretty bewildering. Just move the mouse pointer to each button, and on the title bar you'll see a message about what the button is for.

### *Displaying Another Button Bar*

Click in any button bar with the right mouse button and you'll see a QuickMenu (Figure 1.2). Then pick the button bar you want.

If you don't see *any* button bars on the screen to click on, use this trick: Choose Preferences from the File menu and then double-click on Button Bar.

### *Moving a Button Bar*

Just drag a button bar to move it to another position on the screen. Click on a blank spot on the button bar, and you'll see the pointer change shape to a hand. Drag the bar to a side of the screen to display it along that side (Figure 1.3), or drag it to the middle of the screen if you want the buttons to be displayed as a floating palette (Figure 1.4). Drag it back up to the top of the screen to display it there again.

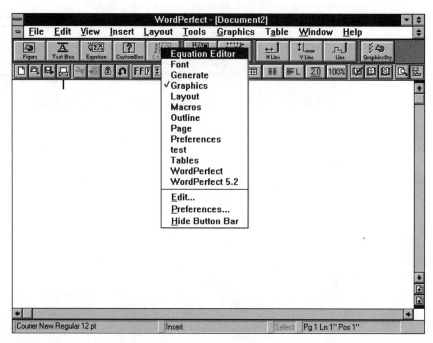

**Figure 1.2** Choosing another button bar

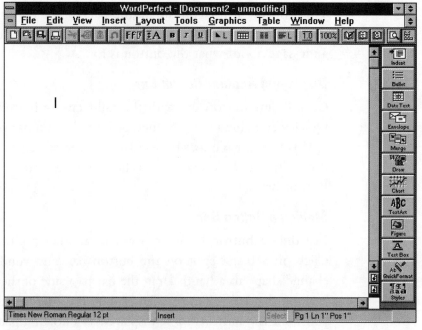

**Figure 1.3** Displaying a button bar on the side

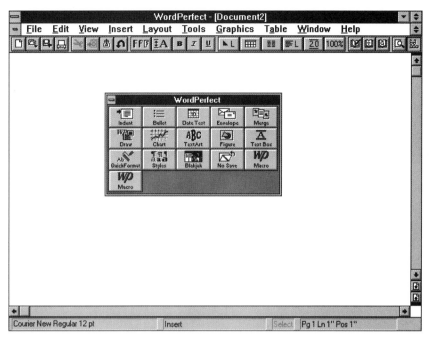

**Figure 1.4**  **Displaying a bar as a floating palette**

### *Moving a Floating Palette*

Drag a floating palette by its title bar, and the button bar won't "stick" to the sides of the screen. You can put it wherever you want without changing it.

### *Using the Power Bar*

The buttons on the power bar (Figure 1.5) give you instant access to the common menu commands. The trick to using the power bar efficiently is to realize that you can click a button to carry out that menu command and *double-click* on many of the buttons to open a dialog box.

Double-click on the Font Face, Font Size, Tab Set, Table Create, Columns Define, Line Spacing, and Zoom buttons to open dialog boxes.

### *Hidden Menus on the Power Bar*

Click and drag on a power bar button to display a pull-down menu you can choose from. You can do this with all the buttons that you can double-click on (see the preceding trick) plus the Justification button.

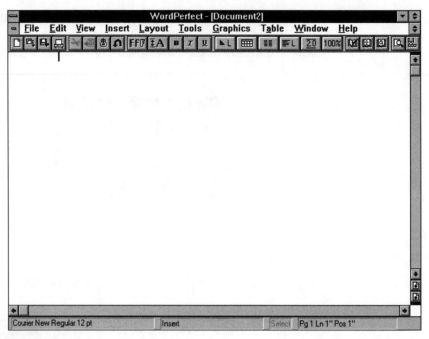

**Figure 1.5**  The power bar

### *What's on the Status Bar?*

The status bar provides a lot of information about your document and has some hidden slick tricks in it, too. Pg is the page number; that's easy enough. Ln is the line number, measured in inches from the top of the page. Pos is for position, and it's the position of the insertion point, again in inches, from the left edge of the page. The status bar also shows the font you're using.

If you're working in a table or in text columns, you'll see the current cell or column on the status bar, too.

### *Double-Click on the Status Bar for Fast Results*

♦ Double-clicking on the name of the font displayed on the status bar takes you to the Font dialog box.

♦ Double-clicking on Insert switches you to Typeover mode.

♦ Double-clicking on the page, line, and position indicators takes you to the Go To dialog box.

### Clicking to Display QuickMenus

You can click with the right mouse button in all sorts of places on the editing screen to display QuickMenus that let you carry out tasks quickly. For example, clicking on the status bar with the right mouse button lets you hide the status bar or set your preferences about using it. Clicking with the right mouse button in text lets you switch fonts, use QuickFormat, run the Speller, or justify or indent text (Figure 1.6). Figure 1.7 illustrates some other places where you can click with the right mouse button to get a QuickMenu. You can also click in a Reveal Codes window with the right mouse button to display a QuickMenu.

### How to Tell if You've Saved the Document

Use the title bar, not the status bar, to see if you've saved the document you're in. Once you save a document, you'll see its filename on the title bar with "unmodified" after it. That means you've saved it and haven't made any changes to it after that. If the title bar just says "unmodified" and doesn't display a filename, you've never saved the document. Better do it now. Press **Ctrl+S**.

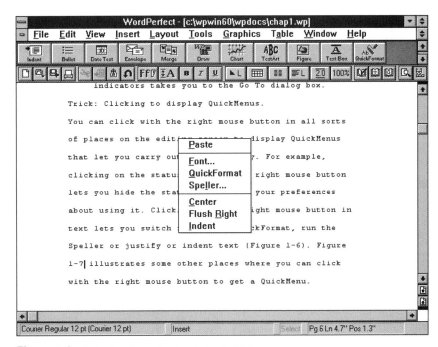

**Figure 1.6** Displaying the text QuickMenu

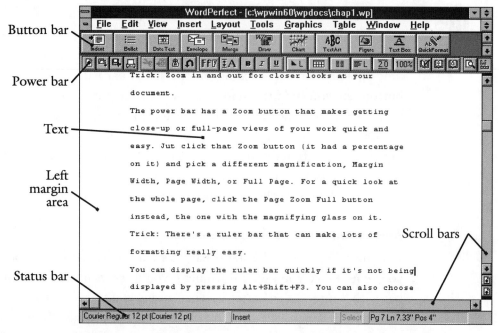

**Figure 1.7** Places where you can click with the right mouse button to get a QuickMenu

### *Zoom Views of Your Document*

The power bar has a Zoom button that makes getting close-up or full-page views of your work quick and easy. Just click that Zoom button (it has a percent sign on it) and pick a different magnification, Margin Width, Page Width, or Full Page. For a quick look at the whole page, click the Page Zoom Full button instead, the one with the magnifying glass icon on it.

### *A Ruler Bar Makes Formatting Easy*

You can display the ruler bar (Figure 1.8) quickly by pressing **Alt+Shift+F3**. You can also choose **R**uler Bar from the **V**iew menu. The ruler bar is really handy for changing margins, setting tabs, and creating special paragraph indents, because you can use the mouse instead of changing settings in dialog boxes. You'll see more about the ruler bar in Chapter 3, "Formatting Tricks."

Here's the trick: You'll probably do most of your document formatting in Page mode, so keep the ruler bar turned off in Draft mode

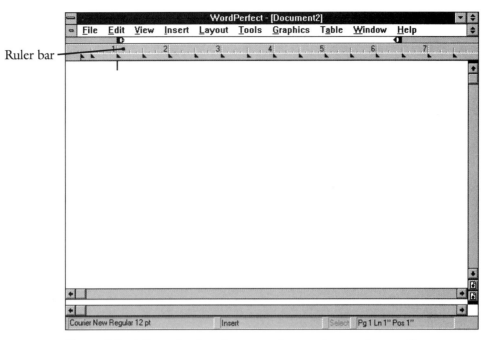

Ruler bar

**Figure 1.8** The ruler bar lets you change formatting easily.

unless you're really using it. You'll have more space to input text in Draft mode.

# Mouse and Keyboard Shortcuts

When should you use the mouse and when the keyboard? The answers depend on how you like to work. If you're already typing, it's often faster to use a keyboard shortcut. But some things in WordPerfect 6.0, such as drag and drop editing, are done faster with the mouse.

### *Choosing from Menus by Using the Keyboard*

If you prefer using the keyboard, you can make menu selections via the keyboard. Press the **Alt** key and type the underlined letter in the menu's name. For example, pressing **Alt** and **F** at the same time opens the File menu. In this book, you'll see pressing two keys at the same time represented as joined by a plus sign (+). For example, pressing **Alt** and typing F will be represented as **Alt+F**.

Then, to select a choice from a menu, type the underlined letter in the menu command's name. Typing n chooses New on the File menu once it's opened, for example. These are called mnemonic shortcuts because they're usually the first letter of the command.

### Using Function Key Shortcuts

If you're used to the function key shortcuts from DOS versions of WordPerfect, rest assured that they're still there. They're based on the Enhanced keyboard in WordPerfect 5.1, so you'll find Help on the **F1** key and Cancel on the **Esc** key. To use those familiar keyboard shortcuts from WordPerfect for DOS, choose **P**references from the **F**ile menu and double-click on the Keyboard option. Then pick the WPDOS compatible keyboard.

---

### Some Key Combinations Are Radically Different

With the DOS keyboard in effect, **Alt+F4** turns on block marking instead of exiting you from WordPerfect. **Shift+F7** is another startler: It takes you to the Print dialog box, instead of centering text. And even though you may have switched to the DOS keyboard, the menus will continue to patiently give you the WordPerfect Windows function-key shortcuts. Ignore them. They don't always work that way on the DOS keyboard.

---

### Use Mnemonic Built-In Keyboard Shortcuts

WordPerfect 6.0 for Windows comes with several wonderfully easy-to-memorize keyboard shortcuts, and if you're just starting out, you'll find them easier to use than any of the program's old standard function-key shortcuts. Here are a few mnemonic shortcuts that are easy to remember:

| | |
|---|---|
| **Ctrl+B** | Bold |
| **Ctrl+C** | Copy |
| **Ctrl+X** | Cut |
| **Ctrl+I** | Italics |

| | |
|---|---|
| **Ctrl+V** | Paste |
| **Ctrl+P** | Print |
| **Ctrl+S** | Save |
| **Ctrl+O** | Open |
| **Ctrl+N** | New Document |
| **Ctrl+Z** | Undo |

These are the same in most other Windows programs, too!

### More Keyboard Shortcuts

WordPerfect 6.0 has even more keyboard shortcuts than you thought, and you can't possibly memorize them all. Here are a few of the most useful ones. They depend on your having a keyboard with 12 function keys:

| | |
|---|---|
| **Alt+F3** | Reveal Codes On/Off |
| **Ctrl+F8** | Margins |
| **Ctrl+W** | WordPerfect Characters |
| **F12** | Table Create |
| **Ctrl+Shift+Q** | QuickMark |
| **F8** | Block on |
| **F3** | Save As |
| **F5** | Print |
| **Alt+F8** | Styles |
| **F9** | Font |

Again, don't try to memorize them all! I'll mention them in connection with specific tricks.

### Repeating a Menu Command

If you want to repeat a command, including a menu command or the click of a button bar, use the handy new Repeat command on the Edit menu. You'll see the dialog box in Figure 1.9. Type the number of times you want the program to repeat your next action. Then click OK and do what you want to do that number of times. You can use this trick to repeat pressing a key, too.

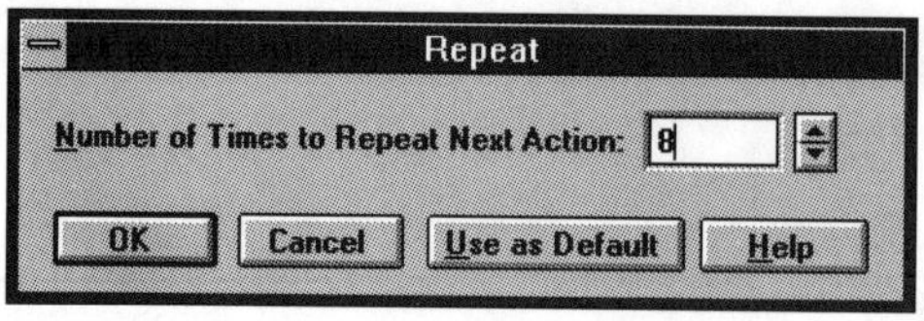

**Figure 1.9** **Repeating an action**

For example, say that you want to open two new documents. Choose Repeat from the Edit menu, type 2, click OK, and click the New document button.

You can also use this trick to move through a document. To move back five pages, use Repeat, enter **5**, click OK, and press the **PgUp** key.

For example, say that you want to open two new documents. Choose Repeat from the Edit menu, type **2**, click OK, and click the New document button.

---

### Shortcuts May Not Always Work

Here's how to reset WordPerfect 6.0 to its factory settings when the shortcuts don't work. Because WordPerfect 6.0 is so customizable, you (or someone else) may have custom-tailored the menus and the keyboard shortcuts. Use this handy trick: Press **Ctrl+Alt+Shift+ Backspace** to restore the default factory-setting menu system if the menus don't seem to be working right.

---

### WordPerfect Has an Undo Command

You can press **Ctrl+Z** (or click the Undo button) to undo the last command you executed. For example, if you've searched for one word, replaced it with another, and then changed your mind, Undo will return the document to the way it was before you searched and replaced. It's wonderful.

There's also an Undelete command that will restore the last three things you deleted. Press **Ctrl+Shift+Z** to use the Undelete shortcut.

Remember, use Undo to undo an editing action; Undelete to restore deleted text. They're both combinations of **Ctrl+Z**, which you can think of as the *wiZard*.

# Working with Windows

WordPerfect lets you have as many as nine different documents open at once, so a few slick tricks will help you manage them.

### *Opening Several Documents at Once*

In an Open dialog box (Figure 1.10), just select the documents you want to open and press **Enter**; **Shift-click** to select documents that are next to each other; and **Ctrl-click** to select individual documents that aren't next to each other.

### *Reopening a Recently Opened Document*

The File menu at the bottom lists the four documents you've opened most recently (Figure 1.11). You can open one of them again quickly by choosing File and then just typing the number next to the document you want to open.

### *Minimize a Document Out of Your Way*

Since WordPerfect lets you have several documents open at once, you may sometimes want to do something with one or two of them so that they don't get in your way. After all, it might be nice to have a lot of documents open, but you probably don't need to be cutting and

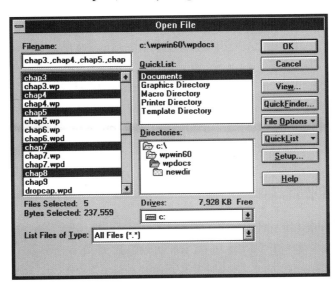

**Figure 1.10** Opening several different documents

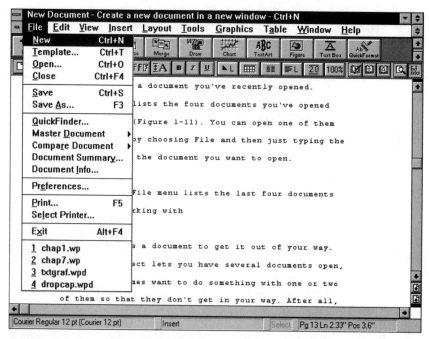

**Figure 1.11** The File menu lists the last four documents worked with.

pasting between *that* many at once. Instead of exiting from all of them so that you have to remember which ones you were working with if you need to get them back, just minimize the ones that you don't need right now to convert them into icons at the bottom of the screen. Reducing a document (see Figure 1.12) gets it handily out of the way by shrinking it, but you can still see into it if you need to copy or cut and paste.

To minimize a document, click its Minimize button. To make it full-screen size (maximize it) again, click its Maximize button. To restore it to the size it was before, click its Restore button. You can also choose Minimize or Maximize from the document's Control menu (**Alt+−** will open the Control menu quickly), but using the buttons is usually faster.

---

### Minimizing a Document Doesn't Save It

You might think that just because something happens to a document when you minimize it, it's been saved. Not so. It's still in memory, ready for you to use. But if you haven't saved it, it's not saved.

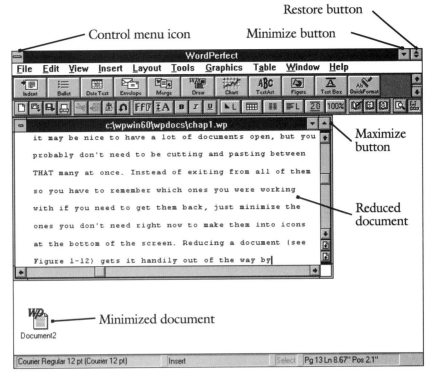

**Figure 1.12** Reducing and minimizing documents

### *Move Reduced Document Windows on the Screen*

Once you've reduced a window, you can drag it by its title bar to reposition it on the screen. This is a handy trick to know if a small document window is covering up text you need to see!

### *Double-Click on the Title Bar for a Full-Screen Window*

Use this handy trick to quickly bring a reduced document window back to full-screen size again: Just double-click on its title bar. If the window's already full-screen size, this will reduce it.

### *Make a Window Any Size*

To resize a window, click in one of its corners. Then drag inward to make the window smaller, or outward to make it larger. You can also drag a window's side borders to resize them. This slick little trick can often help if you need to see more of a particular small window.

### Switching between Documents with Ctrl+F6

Although you can have several documents open, only one of them at a time can be active. If you have several documents open, press **Ctrl+F6** to cycle among them one by one. If you can see the document you want, just click in it to make it active.

### Picking the Window You Want

Instead of cycling through all the windows, choose the one you want to go to from the Window menu. You'll see a list of all the documents that are open (Figure 1.13); choose the one you want.

### Switching between Two Windows Quickly

If you have just a couple of windows open, a quick switch is possible by simply pressing **Shift+F3**; you'll toggle between the two windows.

### Easy Cutting and Pasting: Open Both Documents

If you have a task that requires cutting or copying from one document and pasting in another, open both documents into a window. Then it's easy to switch between them and view them at the same time.

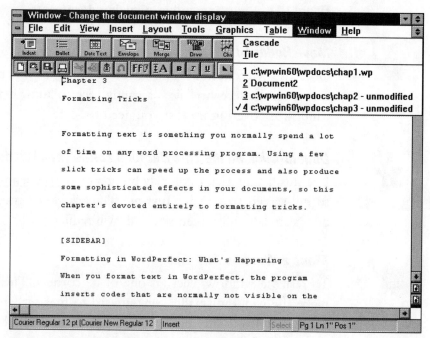

**Figure 1.13** The Window menu lists the documents you have open.

Choose Tile from the Window menu to arrange all your open documents so that you can see into them simultaneously (Figure 1.14).

### Cascade Windows to Stack Them

If you haven't used a Windows word-processing program before, you'll be surprised at all the things WordPerfect 6.0 can do. Tiling and cascading windows are two of these tricks. When you choose **C**ascade from the **W**indow menu, all your open windows are arranged like a pile of cards so that you can see which ones you have open (Figure 1.15).

### When to Tile and When to Cascade

If you're cutting or copying and pasting between documents, tile the windows. Cascade them if you're working in only one window at a time but you want to see which other documents you have open by glancing at their title bars.

### Looking into Two Parts of a Document at Once

Sometimes it's handy to be able to see into two different areas of a document at the same time. Open two copies of the document. Then

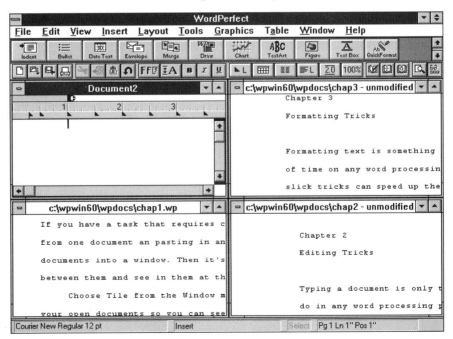

**Figure 1.14**  Tiling windows

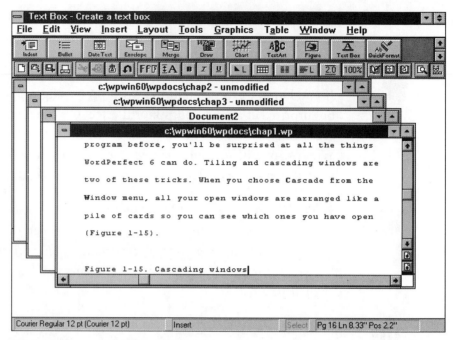

**Figure 1.15**   **Cascading windows**

just be sure to make your changes only in the document that doesn't say "Read-Only" in its title bar. That's the copy. You can really foul things up if you don't pay attention. You'll get a chance to save that copy under another name, but you may not be able to keep track of what you changed. Try using the Compare Document command on the File menu if this happens to you. It happens all too easily.

# Dialog Box Tricks

One basic way WordPerfect 6.0 operates is by using dialog boxes. These are special boxes that request additional information the program needs to be able to do what you want it to. Any time you see a menu choice that has an ellipsis (…) next to it, you'll get a dialog box if you select that item.

There are several different kinds of dialog boxes in WordPerfect: list boxes (where you choose from a list); text boxes (where you have to type text); and check boxes (in which you can choose several options).

And there are command buttons that carry out a command when you choose them (like Close, Exit, and OK) and option buttons that let you pick different features. Figure 1.16 shows a typical dialog box with several of these kinds of boxes and buttons. We'll look at tricks for using these in this section.

### Moving in Dialog Boxes

You can just click with the mouse to move from area to area in dialog boxes. If you'd rather use the keyboard, **Tab** moves you from area to area in a dialog box; **Shift+Tab** moves you backward. You can use the **Up** and **Down arrow** keys, too.

### Cancel a Dialog Box

To get out of a dialog box without making any selections, even if you've already filled out the box, just press **Esc**.

If you'd rather exit from a dialog box by using the mouse instead of the keyboard, try this: Double-click on the dialog box's Close box in the upper left corner. You can click the box's Close button, too.

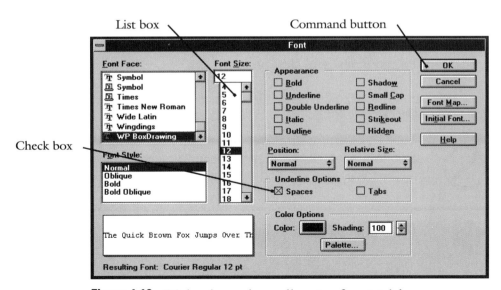

**Figure 1.16** Dialog boxes have all sorts of neat tricks.

### Exit a Dialog Box Before Doing Anything Else

Before you can work in your document again, you usually have to close whatever dialog box you've opened. The program will just move the highlight around the dialog box if you press any keys.

### Drag a Dialog Box Out of Your Way

Sometimes a dialog box can obscure what you're trying to see on the screen. To get it out of your way but keep it handy, just drag it by its title bar to another place on the screen.

### Quick Selecting in List Boxes

In a list, type the first letter of an item's name to move directly to it. The trick is to make the list part of the dialog box active first. For example, if you're looking at the drop-down font list in a Font dialog box (Figure 1.16) and Palatino is the first font beginning with P, you can type p to go straight to Palatino.

### Press Enter to Use a Highlighted Choice

In many dialog boxes, you'll see highlighted buttons, such as the OK button in Figure 1.16. This is the default choice, the one WordPerfect 6.0 is preset to carry out if you don't choose anything else. If you just press Enter, you'll accept that default choice, so you don't have to reach for the mouse and click on it.

### Grayed Items Aren't Available

Sometimes you'll see grayed menu choices and buttons in dialog boxes. That means you can't use them at this time.

### Cut, Copy, and Paste in Text Boxes

If there's text that you want to put into a text box, such as the Search text box, with WordPerfect for Windows you can just copy it from your document and paste it in the box. This is a handy way to avoid typos.

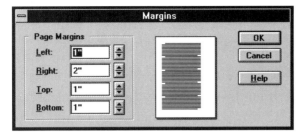

**Figure 1.17** A typical text box

### *Replacing Text in Text Boxes*

You can just start typing to replace what's in a text box: for example, the left margin setting in Figure 1.17. You don't have to delete first and then retype. Overall, this will save you a lot of time.

### *Convert Measurements to Decimal Format*

Don't bother getting out the calculator and converting measurements to inches. You can enter measurements and WordPerfect 6.0 will convert them to decimal format in dialog boxes for you. Just enter a fraction such as $3\frac{2}{3}$ if you want to set a 3.66" left margin, for example, and WordPerfect will figure out the approximate decimal number.

### *Overriding Units of Measurement in Effect*

WordPerfect's factory settings use inches as the standard unit of measurement. You may use centimeters, points (a point is $\frac{1}{72}$ inch), or "WordPerfect units," which are $\frac{1}{1200}$ of an inch and are useful only if you need to fine-tune the placement of graphics. To tell the program that the number you're entering is not in inches, just enter **p** for points, **c** for centimeters, or **w** for WordPerfect units. For example, entering **5p** tells the program "five points," no matter what unit of measurement is in effect. If you've switched from inches to another unit, to tell the program the number you're entering is really in inches, enter the measurement followed by " or **i** for inches.

To change the standard units of measurement, choose Preferences from the File menu and choose Environment.

### Typing Your Way through Dialog Boxes

If you're really a hard-core typist, you may find that typing your way through dialog boxes is faster than reaching for the mouse. You can use the **Tab** or arrow keys to move from area to area. As an alternate way to move around, you can type the mnemonic letter of the choice you want to go to, or type its number. Once you're in that area, use the arrow keys to move to the choice you want to make. Then use the *space bar* to make checks in check boxes. This is easier done than explained. Try it.

If an item's checked, there'll be an X in the box next to it. You can usually check more than one check box in a group.

---

### Select Only One Radio Button at a Time

Only one radio button, unlike check boxes, can be selected in a group. You'll find that out soon enough if you try to choose more than one.

---

### Hidden Drop-Down Lists

In many dialog boxes, there are hidden drop-down lists. These appear when there is a list of items you can choose from, but the dialog box hides the choices most of the time to save space. You can tell that a drop-down list is available if you look closely: There'll be a tiny downward-pointing arrowhead next to the choice. Clicking on the item or on the arrowhead displays the drop-down list (Figure 1.18). You can usually scroll through it or, if you know the first letter of the item you want to choose, just type that letter to go straight to that part of the alphabet.

### Hidden Pop-Up Lists

There are also hidden lists that appear when you choose a pop-up button. These buttons are usually marked by both upward-pointing and downward-pointing arrows (Figure 1.19). Once you've displayed the list, you have to hold the mouse button down to keep it displayed. Drag to your choice and then release the mouse button. Without a mouse, highlight that option by pressing Tab; then press Alt+Down arrow, and

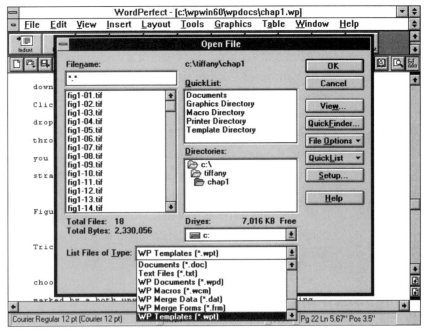

**Figure 1.18** A drop-down list

that will hold the list open for you to type the underlined letter of the choice you want.

### More Arrowheads for Different Things

WordPerfect 6.0 uses arrowheads in dialog boxes to let you change settings, too. These are called increment and decrement arrows, or spin

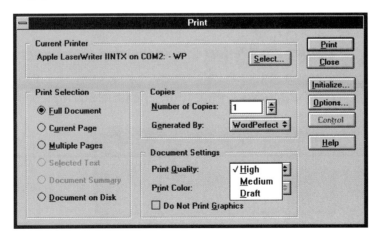

**Figure 1.19** Some dialog boxes have pop-up lists, too.

boxes, but you can forget that. Just remember that if you click on arrows like the ones next to Spacing in Figure 1.20, you'll change the spacing setting a tenth of an inch each time you click. You can just type a new number for that setting, too, which is usually faster. But now you know what those arrows are for and what they're called.

### Work Drop-Down and Pop-Up Lists without a Mouse

To use the keyboard instead of the mouse with a drop-down or pop-up list, type the letter of the command to move to it; then use the arrow keys to move through the list and the **Enter** key to make your choice.

If typing the letter of the command doesn't work, you'll need to press **Tab** to move to that area of the dialog box. Then pressing **Alt+Down arrow** will open the list, as you saw in a previous trick.

## Starting, Saving, Exiting, and All That

Another part of WordPerfect 6.0 that's pretty basic but still lends itself to some mighty slick tricks is simply starting the program, opening documents, saving, and exiting. We'll look at tricks for all that in this section.

### Starting WordPerfect 6.0 from the DOS Prompt

Just type win wpwin to start Windows and WordPerfect 6.0 at the same time from the DOS prompt.

### Starting WordPerfect 6.0 and Opening a Document Simultaneously

This is a fast slick trick to use if you know the name of the document you want to work with. Enter the usual startup command, **win wpwin**,

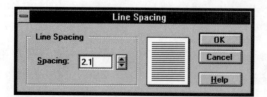

**Figure 1.20** Hidden pop-up (and -down) lists lurk under double arrows.

but follow it with the document's name. For example, if you want to work on a document named CHAP5, enter win wpwin chap5.

If the document isn't stored in your regular documents directory, use the path name to move to its location. For example, if the CHAP5 document is in the directory of C:\WINWORD\DOCS, enter win wpwin c:\winword\docs.

### Starting WordPerfect 6.0 with Its Factory Settings

Ah, this is a neat one to know if you share a computer with another worker who's turned the program into his or her version of how a word processor ought to operate. You can tell WordPerfect 6.0 to start with its factory settings in effect just by giving the startup command as **win wpwin /x**. Remember this one.

### Start WordPerfect 6.0 with Your Personal Setup

If you want to set up WordPerfect 6.0 your way and be able to start it that way, even if you share your computer with other users who have other preferences, use this even slicker trick. Start WordPerfect 6.0 with the command **win wpwin /nt=0**. This tells WordPerfect that you're on a network, even though you're not really connected to one. When the program starts, you'll be asked for your name (up to five characters). Enter your initials. After you're in WordPerfect 6.0, use the Setup menu and format all the other places where you can custom-tailor the program as you want it (see Chapter 4 for details). Now, the next time you start WordPerfect 6.0, use the command **win wpwin /nt=0** and enter your initials when you're asked. WordPerfect 6.0 will start with your preferences in effect.

### Press Ctrl+O to Open a Document Fast

The keyboard shortcut **Ctrl+O** is definitely one worth memorizing. It brings up the Open dialog box right away, without any choosing from menus with the mouse.

There are lots of hidden tricks in an Open dialog box; we'll look at them in Chapter 5.

### Use the Close Command As a Fast Getaway

Choosing **C**lose from the File menu closes the active document immediately. It gives you a chance to save the document if it hasn't been saved. If it's been saved already, you'll get an instant warp-speed close.

---

### Shift+Ctrl+F4 Is a Hidden, Undocumented Clear Shortcut

You can press **Shift+Ctrl+F4** to clear the current document out of the window you're working in, but be careful. This is the same as selecting Close from the File menu, not saving any changes, and then opening the File menu again and selecting New—except it's much faster! If you've made changes to the document but haven't saved it yet, they'll be gone, so use this trick with caution.

---

### WordPerfect 6.0's Closeall and Saveall Macros

The Closeall macro closes all your open documents and gives you a chance to save them if they've been changed but not saved. The Saveall macro saves everything. It's so handy that you may want to make it into a button on your power bar (see Chapter 4 for how to do that), although there's a keyboard shortcut for it, too, as you'll see in a later trick.

To use either one of these macros, press **Alt+F10**, enter closeall or saveall, and press **Enter**.

### Save Your Workspace

You can tell WordPerfect 6.0 to remember the documents you were working on when you saved and exited from the program. Choose **Pref**erences from the File menu. Double-click Environment and choose Always or Prompt on Exit (to be asked if you want the workspace saved each time you exit).

### Quick Saving

To save the document you're working on without any fussy prompting, just press **Ctrl+S**. You won't be asked for a name if it already has one.

To save all the documents you're working on, press **Ctrl+Shift+S**—a very handy shortcut to keep on hand.

### *The Short Goodbye: Exit and Save Everything at Once*

If you've been working on several documents and you're ready to Exit WordPerfect 6.0, don't save each document individually and then exit. There's a faster way. Press **Alt+F4**. You'll get a chance to save all the documents you've been working with, all at once, and then exit.

### *Saving Documents in Other Formats*

If you want to save a document in the format of another word-processing program, or save it under a name that's different from the one it already has, use the Save **A**s command on the **F**ile menu, or press **F3**. You can type a different name for the document or use the drop-down list in the Format box to pick a different format (Figure 1.21).

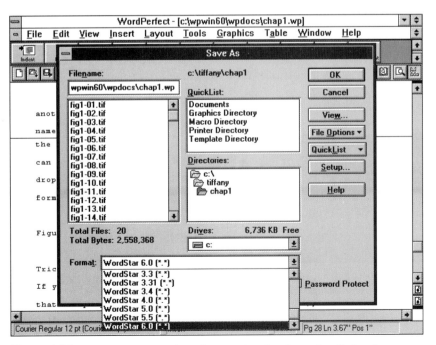

**Figure 1.21**  Choosing another format in the Save As dialog box

### Saving a Document in Another Directory

If you don't want to save the document in the directory that the program is presenting (C:\WPWIN60\WPDOCS in Figure 1.21), just enter the path name to the directory in which you want it saved in the Filename box, instead of opening the directory you want to save it in. For example, to save a document in your WINWORD directory, enter C:\WINWORD followed by a backslash and the document's name.

### Save Blocks of Text, Too

If you've selected a block of text before choosing Save As, WordPerfect 6.0 assumes you want to save just that block, not the whole document. This is a fast way to save a block without copying and pasting into a new editing window and then saving. You'll see a dialog box asking if you want to save the selection or the whole document.

# Getting Help

One of the most basic tricks in any program is being able to get the help you need when you need it. As you might guess, in a complex program like WordPerfect 6.0, there are slick tricks for using Help. There are even built-in *Coaches* that help you learn features of the program, such as Footnotes and Replace.

**Catch Those Coaches**

Coaches take you step by step through the program's features. You'll see exactly when to select text, what step to take next, how to save the changes you make, and so forth. Because Coaches work on the document that you have on the screen, when you've finished you've actually accomplished the task in your document.

To use a Coach, select Coach from the **H**elp menu; then pick which Coach you want to use. WordPerfect Corporation is constantly making more Coaches available. Give them a call to find out if any more have been released since this book was written.

### Use How Do I... Help, Too

There's a new kind of help in WordPerfect 6.0 called How Do I... help. Use this kind of help if you want to know how to do something, such as change margins or use the Speller. To use this new kind of help, choose How Do I... from the Help menu; then pick the topic you want help on. How Do I... help is pretty extensive; try it before you get the manual out and you may save yourself some time.

### Start a Task to Get the Fastest Help on It

If you press **F1** when you have a dialog box open, you'll get context-sensitive help—help about what you're trying to do. So for the fastest, most relevant help, start trying to do what you want to do before you press **F1**, and then you won't have to hunt through the help contents for the topic. For example, if you need help on fonts, open the Font dialog box (**F9**); then press **F1** (Figure 1.22).

### Use the Search Feature in Help

You'll really save a lot of time scrolling if you use the Search for Help On feature of the Help system. Choose Search for Help On from the

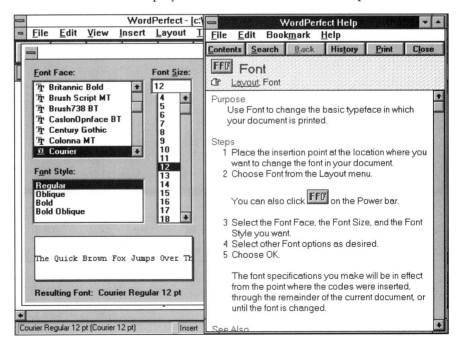

**Figure 1.22** Getting help on fonts

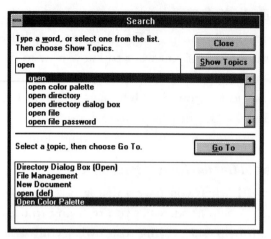

**Figure 1.23**   Double-click on a name to
see related topics.

**H**elp menu; then type in the name of what you need help on and press
**Enter**. Double-clicking on a name from the list will show you related
topics about it (Figure 1.23).

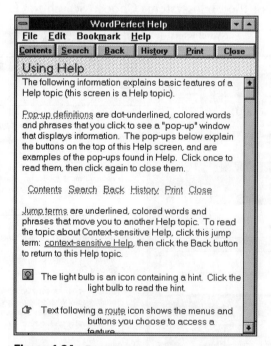

**Figure 1.24**   Jump terms and pop-up
definitions

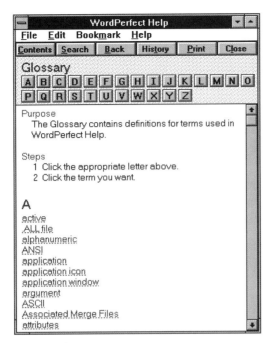

**Figure 1.25** Using the Glossary

### Lost in Help? Here's a Helpful Tip.

As you look for topics in the Help system, you may find yourself at a dead end. If this happens, use the Back button to get back to the topic you just looked at and then start down another branch.

### There Are Hidden Branches in Help

Underlined words on Help screens will take you straight to those topics if you click on them. These are called *jump terms*. Dotted lines indicate pop-up definitions (Figure 1.24).

### Keep a Help Topic Handy; Print It Out

You can print out a help topic directly from the Help system. Just click the Print button while you're looking at the topic.

### Use Help to Identify Your Version of WordPerfect

WordPerfect Corporation constantly releases new interim versions of the program. If you need to see which version date you have, choose

About WordPerfect from the **H**elp menu. Your license number is probably there, too, if you entered it when you installed the program.

If something's not working exactly as described in these tricks, it may be that you have a later release of the program.

### Use Help System's Glossary

If you're really stuck on what you want help for, try looking at the glossary (Figure 1.25). To see it, choose **C**ontents from the **H**elp menu and then choose Glossary. Click on a letter button to get a list of terms beginning with that letter; then double-click on the topic to find out more information about it.

# What Next?

· · · · · · · · · · · · · · · · · · · · · · · · · · · · · · · · · · · · ·

While you use WordPerfect 6.0, you'll spend a great deal of time editing documents you've created—maybe even more time than actually typing the text that's in them. So, Chapter 2 is full of neat slick tricks for typing text and editing, too.

# Chapter 2

· · · · · · · · · · · · · · · · · · · · · · · · · · · · · · · · ·

## Editing Tricks

Typing a document is only the first part of what you do in any word-processing program. Once the document's typed, the real work of editing it begins. You may not think of it as "editing" but instead may consider it fine-tuning, or polishing, or whatever you'd like to call the process of finishing it. Use the slick tricks in this chapter to select text quickly, find what you're looking for, replace one word or phrase with another, copy and cut selections, move through long documents, and more. You'll find all kinds of shortcuts for typing, too, and we'll start with those.

## Typing Tricks

· · · · · · · · · · · · · · · · · · · · · · · · · · · · · · · · ·

WordPerfect 6.0 has all sorts of neat, built-in typing shortcuts, as these tricks will show you.

### Instant Retyping

You absolutely won't have to type the same character over and over again if you use this trick. It's is a great trick for creating dashed lines, for example, where you have to type - - - - - - many times. Just choose Repeat from the Edit menu. Then enter the number of times you want to repeat the character or press **Enter** to accept the default setting of eight times. Now type the character, and it will be repeated as many times as you specified.

You can use this trick with any letter or symbol, or with the number keys to repeat numbers. You can also use it with any of the keystroke combinations that move the cursor.

### Using Special Mode Keys

Some keys and key combinations in WordPerfect 6.0 can toggle you quickly between one mode and another. For example, pressing the **Ins** key toggles between Insert mode, which inserts text between characters, and Typeover, which replaces what's been typed with what you're typing now.

You can also toggle between Insert and Typeover by double-clicking on their names on the status bar.

Other toggle keys:

♦ **Num Lock** lets you type numbers from the numeric keypad.

♦ **Caps Lock** lets you type in capital letters.

### A Good Use for Typeover Mode

About the only thing Typeover is good for is editing data in columns that have equal-sized entries, because you can just type over what's already there without selecting it first.

Watch for "Typeover" on the status line; if you see it, press **Ins** to turn it off or double-click on the word "Typeover."

### Undelete Text Deleted by Mistake

WordPerfect stores the last three things you've deleted, and you can easily get them back by pressing **Ctrl+Shift+Z**. Choose Restore from the dialog box you'll see (Figure 2.1) to put the text at the cursor's position, or choose Previous to restore text you've deleted previously.

You can also click the Undo button to restore the last text you deleted, as long as that was the last thing you did. As soon as you do something else, though, even something as simple as moving the cursor, Undo won't restore deleted text.

**Figure 2.1**  **Restoring deleted text**

### *Use Undelete to Move Deleted Text*

You can delete text and graphics, move the insertion point, and undelete the deleted text there to move it. Use this feature for a slick trick: Undelete text to move or copy it into different locations in the same document, or even in different documents.

---

### *Undelete Doesn't Hold Text Cut with Ctrl-X*

You can paste text that you've cut, but you have to Undelete text that you've deleted. The Undelete buffer stores the last three deletions you made by pressing **Backspace** or **Del**. It doesn't hold text you cut with **Ctrl+X**.

Text that you cut (with **Ctrl+X**) goes to the Clipboard, and you can get it back by pasting.

---

### *Undo Recovers Text Typed Over by Mistake*

If you press **Ins** by mistake and inadvertently turn on Typeover, just use **Ctrl+Z** to recover the text you typed over. If this has ever happened to you, you'll appreciate this simple but slick trick.

### *Ctrl+K Switches Text Case*

Press **Ctrl+K** to quickly switch selected text from lowercase to uppercase, or vice versa. WordPerfect 6.0 has a built-in slick trick that can get you out of trouble if you've pressed **Caps Lock** by mistake, too. Just select the text you typed in all caps by mistake and then press **Ctrl+K**.

WordPerfect 6.0, by default and without your doing anything special, will keep words like I'm and I've (that start with "I") capitalized when you convert from all caps to lowercase.

There's also a Convert Case command on the Edit menu that gives you a little more control over how the words are capitalized (you can choose Initial Capitals, for example), but most of the time **Ctrl+K** is just the shortcut you'll need.

### A Neat Macro Capitalizes the First Letter of a Word

Use the Capital macro to capitalize the first letter of the word the cursor's in. Press **Alt+F10** and enter capital for the fastest way to use it. (For more macro tricks, see Chapter 7.)

### Turn On/Off Formatting with a Keyboard Shortcut

Use the same keyboard shortcut to turn off text formatting that you used to turn it on. Pressing **Ctrl+B** turns on boldface, for example. But did you know that pressing **Ctrl+B** again turns it off? Use this handy keyboard shortcut to switch back to normal text in your document without taking your hands off the keyboard.

## Tricks for Selecting Text

Selecting text is something you do all the time in any word-processing program. WordPerfect 6.0, however, has a lot of built-in shortcuts and secrets for selecting—not just text, but tables, charts, graphics, and other objects.

### Selecting Text with the Keyboard

You can select text with the mouse, the keyboard, or a combination of the two. Selecting with the keyboard is often a much faster technique, because you don't have to take your hands away from it and reach for the mouse.

### Speed Selecting with F8

Press **F8** to turn on Select mode. (You can also double-click on the Select box on the status bar, but then you've already got the mouse in your hand, so why not select with it?) Then use this little trick to extend the highlighting without taking your hands off the keyboard:

♦ To select down one line, press **Down arrow**.

♦ To select up one line, press **Up arrow**.

♦ To select to the next paragraph, press **Ctrl+Down arrow**.

♦ To select the previous paragraph, press **Ctrl+Up arrow**.

♦ To select to the beginning of the document, press **Ctrl+Home**.

♦ To select to the end of the document, press **Ctrl+End**.

♦ To select to the beginning of the line, press **Home**.

♦ To select to the end of the line, press **End**.

There's another, even faster way to do this. Instead of pressing **F8**, press **Shift** and then press any of the key combinations listed above.

Click anywhere else in the document if you change your mind about what you were going to do with that selection; or press **F8** again, or just press an arrow key.

There's also a Select choice on the Edit menu that lets you select the current sentence, paragraph, or page, but selecting with the keyboard or mouse is usually much faster than using that menu. Use it if you need to append text from one document to another (see a later trick in this chapter).

### *Selecting with the Mouse*

OK, you *can* select text with the mouse, and sometimes it's really faster than using the keyboard, especially if you're going back after typing a document to tune up its formatting. Here are a few quick ways to select with the mouse:

♦ Double-click on a word to select it.

♦ Triple-click to select the current sentence.

♦ Click four times to select the current paragraph.

You can also select text by dragging the mouse over it. Click at the beginning of the selection you want to make, then drag the mouse until the text you want is highlighted. This is also faster than selecting with the keyboard if you're selecting irregular areas of text.

### *Bring Up a QuickMenu for Selecting*

There's a hidden QuickMenu in the blank area to the left of the text. Move the mouse pointer over there, and you'll see it change to an arrowhead. Now click with the right mouse button, and you'll get a QuickMenu (Figure 2.2) that lets you select the current sentence, paragraph, page, or the whole document.

### Selecting a Page

If you know that you want to select specific pages—say, from where you are in page 5 to the beginning of page 10—use this trick. Press **F8**; then press **Ctrl+Home** (Go To) and enter the page number you want to go to the beginning of.

To select just the current page, press **Enter** when you see the Go To dialog box.

### Use a Bookmark to Extend a Selection

If you've inserted a bookmark with **Ctrl+Shift+Q**, pressing **F8** and then pressing **Ctrl+Q** extends the selection to that bookmark.

### Instant Paragraph Selecting

For the fastest way to select a paragraph of text, click in it three times with the mouse.

With the keyboard, press **F8**; then press **Ctrl+Up arrow** or **Ctrl+ Down arrow** to select paragraph by paragraph.

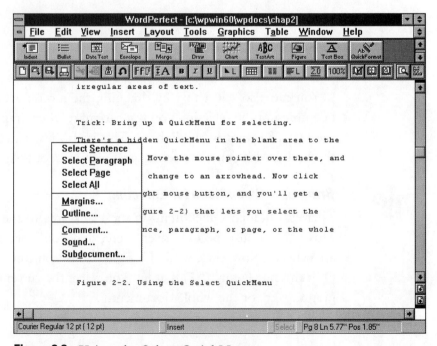

**Figure 2.2**  Using the Select QuickMenu

### Selecting a Line of Text

Move the pointer to the left of the text, and you'll see it change to an arrowhead. Now click, and the line's selected. Just drag to select more lines.

With the keyboard, press **F8**; then press the **Up** or **Down arrow** keys to select line by line.

### Selecting Single Characters

Often, you'll want to select just one character. Trying to hit that tiny target with the mouse can get really tedious, so remember this keyboard trick. Instead of reaching for the mouse, with the insertion point next to the character you want to select, press **F8** and then the **Right** or **Left arrow** key.

### Selecting Word by Word

Press **F8**; then just press **Ctrl+Right arrow** or **Ctrl+Left arrow** to select the word to the right or left of the insertion point. If the insertion point is in the middle of a word, you'll select only to the beginning or end of the word. Keep pressing an arrow key with the **Ctrl** key held down to keep on selecting word by word.

### Using Find to Extend a Selection

If you want to extend a selection to a specific part of the text that's not visible on the screen, use the Find command to locate that word or phrase so that you don't have to scroll to find it. It's much faster than scrolling!

First, click at the beginning of the text you want to select. Then press **F2** and type the word or phrase to which you want to extend the selection. From the Find dialog box's Action menu (Figure 2.3), choose Extend Selection and press **Enter** to find the next occurrence.

### Append Text to the Clipboard to Build Documents

When text or graphics has been selected in a document, you can use the Append command on the Edit menu to add a copy of whatever's selected to the Clipboard, instead of replacing what's already there. It's a great way to create one document from another, take notes, or compile

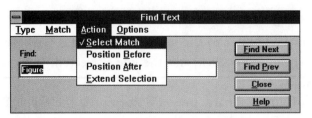

**Figure 2.3**   Choose Extend Selection to use
Find to extend a selection.

footnote reference material into another document so that you can look
up the exact references later. You can even append names, phone numbers, recipes, or quiz answers to lists.

### *Copying Selections*

Hold down the **Ctrl** key while you drag to make a copy of what you've
selected, instead of moving it. This is a great hidden slick trick.

**Dragging and Dropping**   Dragging and dropping is a quick and easy way to copy
or move text. All you need to do is select the text you
want to copy or move; then put the cursor anywhere in
the selection, press the left mouse button, and drag the text to its
new location. When you have it where you want it, release the
mouse button.

When drag and drop is enabled, the cursor changes to an arrowhead with a tiny box showing where the text will appear if you click
in that location.

Normally, WordPerfect moves text that you drag and drop. If you
want to copy it instead, press the **Ctrl** key as you drag.

Until you get used to dragging and dropping (it takes a little practice), you may wind up with text in places that aren't quite where you
wanted it. To undo a drag-and-drop operation and put the text back
where it came from, don't try to drag it back: Just press **Ctrl+Z** for
Undo.

### Turning Off a Selection

After you've dragged and dropped text, it stays selected. To turn off the selection, just click the mouse button. You can also press **F8** or press an arrow key to deselect it, too.

### QuickMenu for Copying, Cutting, and Pasting

If you like to drag and drop rather than use the keyboard, you'll probably like to use a QuickMenu for copying, cutting, deleting, and pasting, too. Make a selection; then press the right mouse button, and you'll get a QuickMenu (Figure 2.4) for these operations.

### Shortcuts for Cutting, Copying, and Pasting

If you don't use any other keyboard shortcuts in WordPerfect 6.0, use these:

**Ctrl+C**    Copy

**Ctrl+X**    Cut

**Ctrl+V**    Paste

They're much faster than using menus.

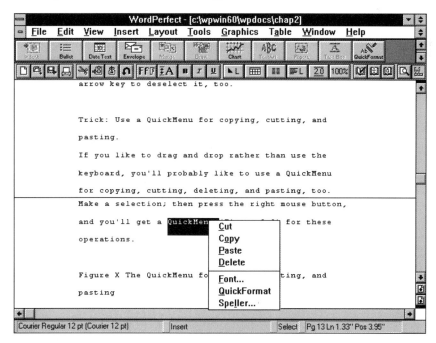

**Figure 2.4**   The QuickMenu for copying, cutting, and pasting

### Shortcuts for Deleting Text

WordPerfect has several built-in shortcuts for deleting text with the keyboard. Here are the easiest ones:

- ♦ To delete a word, put the cursor in it and press **Ctrl+Backspace**.
- ♦ To delete a line, put the cursor at the beginning of the line and press **Delete**.
- ♦ To delete from the cursor to the end of a line, press **Ctrl+Del**.
- ♦ To delete from the cursor to the end of the page, press **Ctrl+Shift+Del**.

# Finding Your Place

Just as important as selecting text, if you're working in a big document, is being able to move around in it. Here are all sorts of tricks to help you get around.

### Move Quickly to the Start or Finish of a Document

The absolutely fastest way to go to the beginning or end of a document is to press **Ctrl+Home** and **Ctrl+End**, respectively. Remember those combinations.

### Bring Up the Go To Dialog Box

Pressing **Ctrl+G** displays the Go To dialog box (Figure 2.5), where you can type the page number you want to go to. You can also right-click on a scroll bar or double-click on the Pg box on the status bar to get to the Go To dialog box.

### Returning to Where You Were

Press **Ctrl+G**, **Alt+P**, and **Enter** to get right back to where you came from. This opens the Go To dialog box, chooses Last Position, and carries out the action.

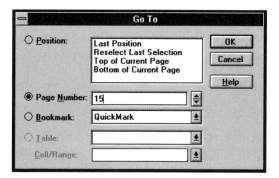

**Figure 2.5**  Using the Go To dialog box

### Selecting the Whole Document May Lose Your Place

After you select the entire document to change the font, switch to a different line spacing, or do something like that, you'll wind up back at the beginning of the document when the operation's over. So if you want to get back to where you were, set a bookmark (press **Ctrl+Shift+Q**) before you Select All. Then you can use **Ctrl+Q** to get back to where you were.

### Scroll Bars Can Move You, Too

Dragging the scroll box location is often the fastest way to go if you're not sure of the page number you want to go to, but think you want to wind up somewhere in the middle of the document, in the first quarter of it, somewhere near the end, and so forth.

Drag all the way to the top of the bar if you want to go to the beginning of your document, or all the way to the bottom to go to its end.

### Scrolling Line by Line

If you want to move line by line through a document, simply press the **Down arrow** key. If you've already got the mouse in your hand, click repeatedly on the tiny arrowheads at the top and bottom of the scrollbars.

### Quick Mouse Scrolling

Just drag downward or upward through the text. When you get to the top or bottom of the window, the text will scroll.

## Insertion Point Doesn't Move When You Scroll

When you use the scroll bars to move through a document, the insertion point stays where it was. If you start typing without clicking in your new location, WordPerfect 6.0 displays the page where the insertion point is and inserts the text you type there. So if you scroll, be sure to click to reset the insertion point before you start typing.

### Move through Text with Keyboard Shortcuts

Here are several keyboard shortcuts for moving through documents:

| To Move | Press |
| --- | --- |
| Word by word | **Ctrl+Right arrow** and **Ctrl+Left arrow** |
| Line by line | **Right arrow** and **Left arrow** |
| Paragraph by paragraph | **Ctrl+Up arrow** and **Ctrl+Down arrow** |
| Page by page | **Alt+PgUp** and **Alt+PgDn** |
| Screen by screen | **PgDn** and **PgUp** |
| End or beginning of a line | **End** or **Home** |

### Use the Numeric Keypad for Cursor Movement

If **Num Lock** hasn't been pressed, you may use the numeric keypad as cursor-movement keys. The light above the numeric keypad on most keyboards tells you whether Num Lock is on or off. A sure sign that it is on is that you get numbers when you use the numeric keypad!

To turn off Num Lock when you start your computer if you're running DOS 6, put the statement NUMLOCK OFF in your CONFIG.SYS file.

### Use a Bookmark to Find Your Place

WordPerfect has a built-in Bookmark feature you can use to mark your place. There are two kinds of bookmarks—QuickMarks and Bookmarks. A QuickMark is a generic bookmark, and you can have only one of them per document. If all you want to do is mark one place in a document, set a QuickMark so that you can get back there quickly.

♦ Press **Ctrl+Shift+Q** to set a QuickMark quickly with the keyboard. You won't see anything on the screen, but a hidden code is put in your document at the cursor's position.

♦ To find that QuickMark again, press **Ctrl+Q**.

### Going Back to Where You Stopped Working

You can immediately go back to where you stopped working when you saved a document if you set a QuickMark at that location. When you open the document again, just press **Ctrl+Q** to go to that QuickMark.

Remember this one; it's a real timesaver if you work in long documents.

You'll see in Chapter 4 how to make WordPerfect 6.0 automatically mark your place each time you save and close a document.

### Use Bookmarks for Multiple Markers

If there are several locations you need to mark in a document, you can use several bookmarks. This can save you a lot of time if you find that you're constantly jumping around from place to place.

Just put the insertion point at the spot you'd like to mark, or select the text you want to go back to if you want it to be selected when you get there. Choose **B**ookmark from the **I**nsert menu or right-click on a scroll bar and choose Bookmarks. Then choose **Create** and type a short name that helps you remember what the bookmark's for.

To go back to the place you marked, choose **B**ookmark from the **I**nsert menu and double-click on your bookmark's name (Figure 2.6).

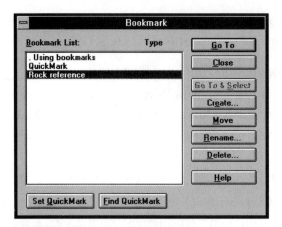

**Figure 2.6**  Using bookmarks

### *Select Text before You Set a Bookmark*

If you select text before you make a Bookmark, that text will be selected again when you find it. This is a handy tip if you're copying or cutting text in different locations, because your selection comes up ready for you to use.

# Searching, and Searching and Replacing

If you know that a certain word or phrase is somewhere in your document, searching for it directly is usually the fastest way to find it, instead of scrolling through the document and trying to read what's on the screen. But you can do much more than simply find things with Word-Perfect's search and search-and-replace features. For example, you can remove all occurrences of something from a document ("strip it out") by searching for it and replacing it with nothing. You can search for format codes, too, not just text. And WordPerfect 6.0 even lets you search for specific code settings, such as a code that switches to a specific font and size.

To search, press **F2**, enter what you're searching for, and press **Enter**. To search and replace, start with **Ctrl+F2**.

### *Searching for a Specific Word*

If you enter wood, WordPerfect 6.0 locates words such as *woody, Woodman, woodsy,* and so forth. But all you want to find is *wood*! Here's a tip for locating a specific word in a document: Press the space bar to put a space before and after the word, or choose Whole Word from the Match menu in the Find Text dialog box (Figure 2.7).

It's safer to choose Whole Word than to use the trick with the spaces, because the word you're looking for may have a comma, period, or other punctuation after it. But the space trick works most of the time and is faster.

### Search Shortcuts

Press **Shift+F2** to search for the next occurrence of what you just searched for without opening the Find dialog box. Press **Alt+F2** to search backward for the previous occurrence of what you searched for. This trick makes it much easier to see what's on the screen as you search, with no dialog box in the way.

### Searching for Codes

While you're in the Find Text dialog box, you may insert codes to have WordPerfect 6.0 search for them. Choose Codes from the Match menu to see a list of codes you can search for (Figure 2.8). Double-click on a code's name to insert it in the Find box.

### Search for a Specific Code, Too

If you want to locate a code that switches to a specific font in your document, instead of searching for all the font-change codes, use this trick. Choose **S**pecific Codes from the **T**ype menu. Select the code you want to look for and fill in the specific value you want WordPerfect to locate. If you're looking for a font, choose the font you want to find (Figure 2.9).

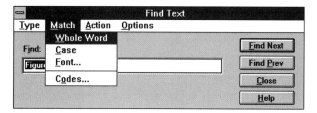

**Figure 2.7**   Matching a whole word

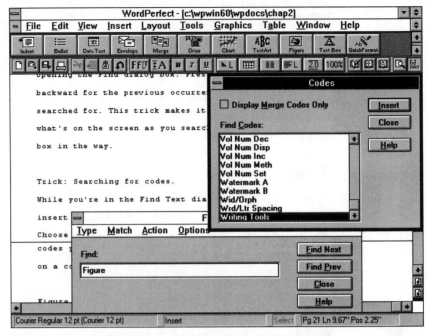

**Figure 2.8**   A partial list of codes you can search for

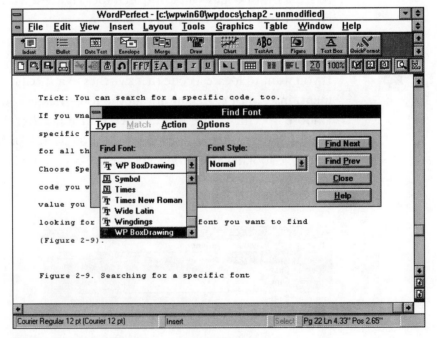

**Figure 2.9**   Searching for a specific font

### Search for a Unique Word

To keep your searches quick, try to keep the search pattern as unique as you can. If you search for a common word like *the* or *also,* you're guaranteed to find a lot of them, which just slows down the search process. If you're not sure exactly what word to search for, use wildcards. The wildcard code **?** represents any one character or none at all, and the code **\*** represents any number of characters or none at all. You can choose these codes by selecting Codes from the **M**atch menu.

For example, if you want to search for a company name that's something like *Industrial* or *Industries* or *Independent,* but you can remember only part of it, try searching for *Ind\*.*

### Search for Special Characters, Too

You can search for WordPerfect characters by simply pressing **Ctrl+W** when the cursor is in the Find box. You'll see the WordPerfect Characters dialog box, where you can choose the character set that has the character you want to search for. Then just double-click on the character to put it in the Find box.

### Safe Replacing

If you click the Replace All button in the Find and Replace Text dialog box (Figure 2.10), WordPerfect 6.0 will go ahead and replace everything you specified with the new text you specified. Sometimes you can get bizarre results, because the program will carry out exactly what you tell it to do. If, for example, you tell it to locate *man* and replace it with *woman*, you may get unusual compound words like *workwoman* (instead of workman) and proper nouns like *Womannheim* (instead of Mannheim). It's safest to confirm each replacement as the program

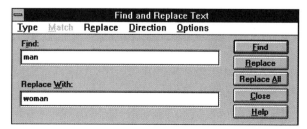

**Figure 2.10** Finding and replacing

finds it. To do this, click Find first; then, if what the program finds is something you want replaced, click Replace. If something slips past you, use the next tip.

### Reverse the Effects of a Search-and-Replace

If you replace by mistake all the occurrences of something with something you didn't intend, you can Undo the search-and-replace operation by pressing **Ctrl+Z** (or clicking the Undo button) as soon as the operation is over and you see that it didn't do what you wanted.

If you do something else, such as reformatting a paragraph or deleting a word, before you use Undo, *that* operation is the one that will be undone, not your search-and-replacement. Undo undoes just the last thing you did. So look over your text after searching and replacing to make sure things turned out the way you intended, before you do anything else.

### Use Replace to Strip Out Text and Codes

A quick way to remove all occurrences of something from a document is to search for it and replace it with nothing. For example, if you want to remove all the italics from a document, search for the [Italic On] code and keep the Replace With box empty.

### The Abbreviations Feature Expands Abbreviations

You can use the program's search-and-replace feature to replace abbreviations you use in a document with a spelled-out version of what you want, but WordPerfect also has a built-in Abbreviations feature that you can use to expand abbreviations. Using abbreviations with either of these features can save you a lot of typing time in a big document that uses hard-to-spell names like *Zamczyk* or long names like *Consolidated Freightways, Incorporated*.

1. Type the full name or phrase that you want to abbreviate. Then select it.

2. Choose **Abbreviations** from the Insert menu; then choose Create (Figure 2.11).

3. Type the abbreviation you want to use; then click OK and Close.

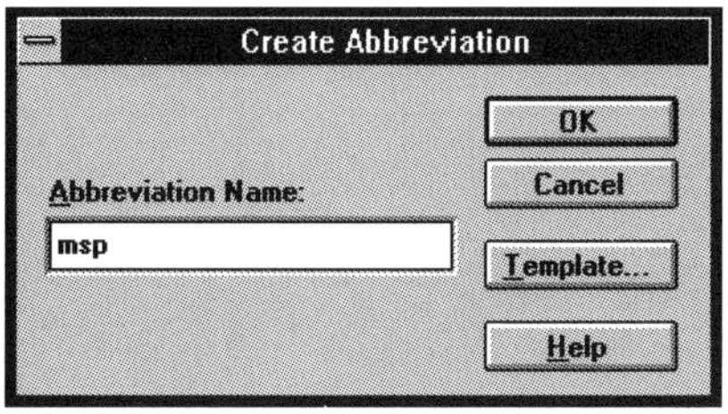

**Create Abbreviation**

OK

Cancel

Abbreviation Name:

msp

Template...

Help

**Figure 2.11** **Setting up an abbreviation**

Now, as you type your document, just type the abbreviation and press **Ctrl+A** and the abbreviation will expand.

You can wait until you're through typing and then go back and expand that abbreviation every time it occurs by selecting it in the Abbreviations dialog box and clicking Expand. But if you use several abbreviations in a document, you'll find the next trick's faster.

### *Expand All Abbreviations in a Document*

If you'd rather type a document and then go back and expand all the abbreviations in it, all at once, type the document using abbreviations. Then go to the beginning of the document, press **Alt+F10**, enter **expndall**, and press **Enter**. This runs a special EXPNDALL macro that comes with the program.

# What Next?

• • • • • • • • • • • • • • • • • • • • • • • • • • • • • • • •

After the chores of inputting and editing, of course, comes formatting—which is what all the slick tricks in the next chapter are about.

# Chapter 3

· · · · · · · · · · · · · · · · · · · · · · · · · · · · · · ·

## Formatting Tricks

FORMATTING TEXT IS SOMETHING you normally spend a lot of time on in any word-processing program. Using a few slick tricks can speed up the process and also produce some sophisticated effects in your documents, so this chapter's devoted entirely to formatting tricks.

### Delete Codes with Reveal Codes Window Open

You can add and delete text, too, with the Reveal Codes window open, *in the Reveal Codes window*. You can click in the Reveal Codes window to move the cursor. Often, it's much easier to target the codes you want to delete in the Reveal Codes window instead of in the regular editing window.

### Want a Bigger Reveal Codes Window? Resize It.

Normally the program opens a Reveal Codes window that's about one-fourth the size of the screen. If you're doing a lot of tedious formatting, you may want a larger view. Just drag the split bar (Figure 3.1) between the two windows. (If the Reveal Codes window isn't open, the split bar is the dark bar just above the vertical scroll bar.) You can have a different

## Formatting in WordPerfect: What's Happening

When you format text in WordPerfect, the program inserts codes that are normally not visible on the screen. For example, pressing **Enter** produces a hard return [HRt] code. To see these codes, press **Alt+F3** or choose Reveal **C**odes from the **V**iew menu. A new window will open at the bottom of the screen. Press **Alt+F3** again to close that window, or drag the line that separates it from the text to make the window a different size.

In Page views, you see text formatted as it will appear when it's printed, so you usually don't need to worry about viewing hidden codes. In Draft mode, though, you may often want to take a peek at the hidden codes the program is using.

Sometimes you won't see everything that's in a code, because WordPerfect isn't displaying all the codes to save space. To check on absolutely everything that's in a code, click on the code. A code such as [Ln Spacing] will expand to show you that it's really [Ln Spacing: 1.0] or whatever its specific settings are.

WordPerfect normally uses a system called Auto Code Placement to put these codes in your document. With Auto Code Placement, codes that affect the entire paragraph are placed at the beginning of the paragraph; codes that affect the entire page are placed at the beginning of the page. For example, if you change the right margin setting for a paragraph, that code appears before the first text in the paragraph, not at the cursor's position where you changed the margin. Likewise, if you pick a border for a page, that code appears at the beginning of the page instead of at the cursor's position.

size for *each* document you have open (or have it open in some documents but not all of them), which is convenient for looking at codes in some documents but not in others.

To change the default size of the Reveal Codes window so that it's larger or smaller than 25% of the screen in all the documents you open, choose Preferences from the File menu, double-click on Display, click Reveal Codes, and set a different window size (Figure 3.2).

To see codes in detail all the time, too, click Show Codes in Detail.

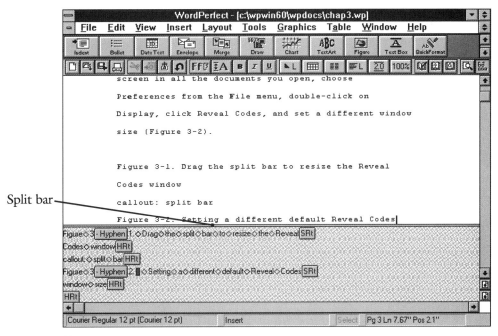

Split bar

**Figure 3.1** Drag the split bar to resize the Reveal Codes window.

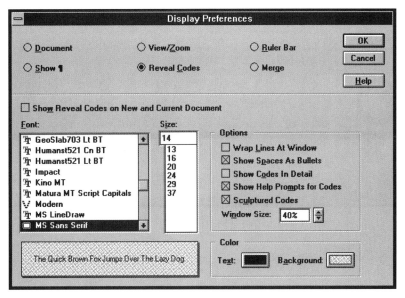

**Figure 3.2** Setting a different default Reveal Codes window size

**Initial Styles**

WordPerfect 6.0 uses a system called an *initial style* to control the default settings in your documents. If you've used earlier versions of the program, you may recall that the feature was called Initial Codes.

Basically, the way that the initial style works is that you insert all the codes you want to use in all the documents you create. You do this by choosing the commands that generate these codes in a special dialog box called the Styles Editor. To reach the Styles Editor quickly, go to the top of your document, open the Reveal Codes window, and double-click on the [Open Style: Initial codes] code. After you read the tricks in this chapter, you may want to set up your own custom initial style by using some of the formatting settings you'll discover here.

### Instant Code Editing: Double-Click on a Code

If you want to change one code to another, simply double-click on the code in the Reveal Codes window. You'll go to the dialog box that lets you change that code to another one. For example, if you want to change from single to double line spacing, double-click on a [Ln Spacing] code and you'll go straight to the Line Spacing dialog box.

### Some Codes Can't Be Deleted without Opening a Reveal Codes Window

WordPerfect won't let you delete some formatting codes unless you've opened the Reveal Codes window. If you've used earlier versions of the program, you may find this annoying. To have WordPerfect prompt you to confirm that you really want to delete a code instead of requiring you to open a Reveal Codes window, choose Preferences from the File menu. Double-click Environment and check the Confirm Deletion of Codes; Stop Insertion Point At Hidden Codes box (Figure 3.3). Then choose OK and Close.

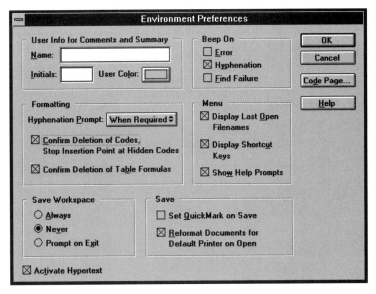

**Figure 3.3** Telling WordPerfect you want to be prompted when you delete a code

### Use the Initial Style Feature to Create Default Settings

Say, for example, that you want all your documents to be double-spaced instead of single-spaced. Instead of changing the line spacing each time you begin a new document, just choose **Document** from the **Layout** menu and choose Initial Codes **S**tyle. You'll see the Styles Editor (Figure 3.4), where you can set up the style you want to use. Click the Use as Default box to use that style in all the new documents you create.

Any "local" formatting you do—such as switching to a different line spacing, changing justification, and so forth—overrides the settings of whatever initial style you set. For example, you might want to change margins or line spacing, choose Left justification, and so forth. You can override these settings in any document just by choosing new ones.

### Change the Initial Font, Too

You can change the initial font for the document you're working on without changing the initial style. Just press **F9** and click the Initial Font button, which opens the Document Initial Font dialog box (Figure 3.5).

If you want that font to be the font used in *all* the documents you create, click the Set as Printer Initial font box.

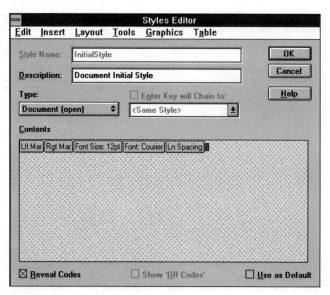

**Figure 3.4**  Specifying default formatting settings
in an initial style

### *Skip Pages with Delay Codes*

Now, this is a slick and rather sophisticated trick. WordPerfect lets you
insert special Delay codes that don't take effect either at the cursor's
position *or* at the beginning of the paragraph or page, but instead take

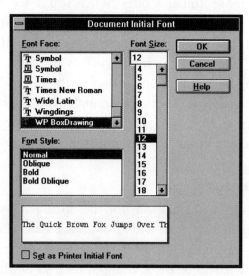

**Figure 3.5**  Specifying an initial font

effect on the page that you specify. For example, if you normally print your letters on preprinted letterhead, you can at the beginning of the document set up a paper size for the second page, where you want to switch to regular blank paper, but insert the page-size change as a delay code so that it won't take effect until the second page.

To create a Delay code, choose **P**age from the **L**ayout menu; then choose **D**elay Codes and enter the number of pages to skip (Figure 3.6). Be sure to enter the number of pages to *skip*, rather than the page number you want the change to occur on. For example, if you're on page 2 and you want the change to take place on page 3, enter **1**.

When you see the Delay Codes editing window and feature bar (Figure 3.7), click the button for the commands that will create the codes you want to insert. For example, to pick a different page size, you'd choose **P**aper Size.

In addition to changing the paper size, you can insert a figure, set up a different header or footer, or set up a watermark as a Delay code to take effect later in a document, after the current page.

## Tricks for Easy Character Formatting

· · · · · · · · · · · · · · · · · · · · · · · · · · · · · · · · · ·

WordPerfect has several hidden, built-in shortcuts for formatting characters.

### *Ctrl Key Shortcuts for Italics, Underlining, and Boldface*

The built-in shortcuts **Ctrl+B** for boldface, **Ctrl+U** for underlining, and **Ctrl+I** for italics are easy to remember and quick to use. You can also select text and click the bold, italic, or underline buttons on the power bar.

**Figure 3.6**  Setting the number of pages to delay

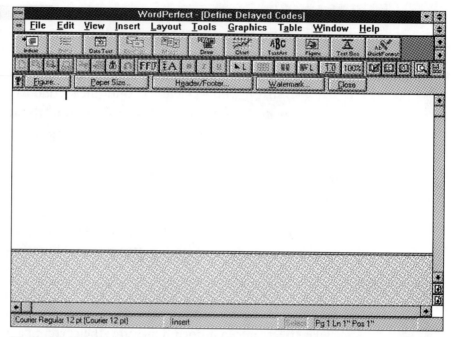

**Figure 3.7**  The Delay Codes feature bar and editing window

### *Returning to Regular Text Quickly*

To return to regular (normal) text, press the **Right arrow** key when you're ready to start typing normal text again. This moves the cursor off the invisible code that controls the text's appearance.

You can also use the same shortcut key or button you originally used to turn off a special text appearance. For example, if you've pressed **Ctrl+B** to turn on boldface, pressing **Ctrl+B** again turns it off. So, to bold just one letter in a word as you type, press **Ctrl+B**, type the letter, press **Ctrl+B** again and keep on typing.

### *Shortcuts to the Font Dialog Box*

These are handy shortcuts that are worthwhile memorizing. Pressing **Ctrl+F** or **F9** takes you straight to the Font dialog box (Figure 3.8). So does clicking in text with the right mouse button and choosing Font.

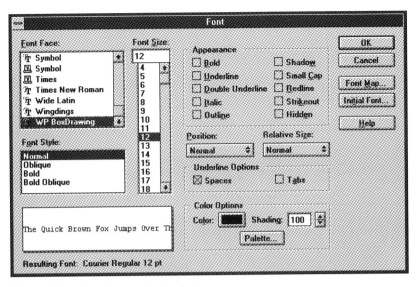

**Figure 3.8** The Font dialog box

# Creating Special Characters

WordPerfect 6.0 comes with a huge range of special characters. It has 15 character sets containing over 1400 special characters and symbols. Instead of handling these characters like other word-processing programs do—which make you switch to a certain font and then choose a character from it—you can access these symbols and special characters while you're using any font in WordPerfect. That's a pretty slick trick in itself.

### Ctrl+W Shows WordPerfect Character Sets

All you need to do to access these 1400+ special characters is press **Ctrl+W**. You'll see the WordPerfect Characters dialog box (Figure 3.9). Pick a character set (click next to Set) and double-click on a character to put it in your document. This is a place where it's very handy to have a mouse. WordPerfect remembers the last character set you used and shows it to you next time you press **Ctrl+W**.

### Multinational and Typographic Symbols Character Sets

Most likely, any symbol you're looking for will be in either the Multinational set (set 1) or the Typographic Symbols set (set 4). Don't bother looking through the others unless you're searching for an arcane

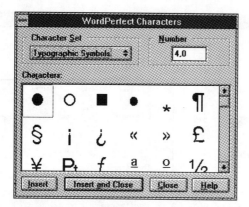

**Figure 3.9** The WordPerfect
Characters dialog box

mathematical symbol (check out sets 6 and 7). Here are all of the
character sets, so you'll know where to look in a search for a strange
character:

| | |
|---|---|
| ASCII (typewriter symbols) | Set 0 |
| Multinational | Set 1 |
| Phonetic | Set 2 |
| Box Drawing (single and double lines) | Set 3 |
| Typographic Symbols | Set 4 |
| Iconic Symbols (happy faces, etc., including dingbats) | Set 5 |
| Math/Scientific | Set 6 |
| Math/Scientific Extension (large characters) | Set 7 |
| Greek | Set 8 |
| Hebrew | Set 9 |
| Cyrillic | Set 10 |
| Japanese | Set 11 |
| User Defined | Set 12 |
| Arabic | Set 13 |
| Arabic Script | Set 14 |

### Enter Character Set Numbers Manually

If you know the character set number and character number of the symbol you want, you can enter it in the Number part of the WordPerfect Characters dialog box, which is often faster than picking from the symbol sets.

Press **Ctrl+W** and then enter the set number, a comma, and the character number. For example, to get an acute e (é) from the Multinational character set 1, enter **1,41**.

How do you determine a character's number? Display the set and count. Keep a list of the symbols you use often. If you use any of them *a lot*, consider recording them as macros or make a button for them.

### Create Symbols Quickly

Even slicker trick: To get a special character, press **Ctrl+W** and type a combination of symbols. WordPerfect "knows" some slick shortcuts for producing commonly used symbols. You can learn these, too, and create symbols very quickly, without memorizing character numbers or using a dialog box. (See Table 3.1.) You can substitute any vowel (a, e, i, o, u) for the *a* in the table.

Press **Ctrl+W** first, then enter the characters in the second column. Click the Insert button or double-click on the symbol to insert it in your document.

### Em and En Dashes for a Professional Touch

If you look at Table 3.1, you'll see two unusual "hyphens." These are the em dash (the big one) and the en dash (the little one). En dashes are a little longer than regular hyphens; they're often used as minus signs. To be proper and correct, use an en dash to indicate a range of numbers, as in "during 1981–82" or "see pages 41–55."

Em dashes are long dashes—like the one you see here. For a professional, typeset look to your documents, use these symbols the way you see them in this book, with no space around them and the proper symbol in the proper place.

If you use em and en dashes (or any other symbol) often, make a macro or button for them and then just click on the button or play the macro to insert the symbol. See Chapter 4 for how to make a procedure into a button.

## Table 3.1   Creating Symbols Quickly

| To Create | Press |
| --- | --- |
| ä | a" |
| â | a^ |
| á | a' |
| à | a' |
| ç | c, |
| © | co |
| ® | ro |
| • | ** |
| £ | L- |
| ¡ | !! |
| ¿ | ?? |
| ½ | /2 |
| ¼ | /4 |
| » | >> |
| « | << |
| ≥ | >= |
| ≤ | <= |
| ± | +- |
| – | n- |
| — | m- |
| ™ | tm |
| ℞ | rx |
| ß | ss |

### Instant Bulleted and Numbered Lists

If all you want is a bullet, just click on the Bullet button on the Word-Perfect button bar. You'll see a dialog box (Figure 3.10) where you can pick the kind of bullet you want.

To create a bulleted or numbered list instantly (almost), type the text you want to have in the list, pressing **Enter** after each item. Then select the text and click the Bullet button. Pick the style you want and click OK. WordPerfect will number the items correctly for you if you've chosen a numbered list. (See Chapter 7 for a few more bullet tricks.)

### Use Hidden Text for Document Comments

One special text appearance that's often overlooked is hidden text. Everybody knows about boldfacing, underlining, and even small caps and strikeout, right? But WordPerfect also lets you make text hidden so that it will appear on the screen but won't normally be printed out. This is a great way to put comments in documents that are circulating among several different people for review. Or say that you're a teacher preparing a test complete with an answer key. Sometimes you'll want to print the test with the answer key; sometimes without.

- ♦ To hide text, select it; then press **F9**. Check the Hidden box in the Font dialog box.
- ♦ To view (or not view) hidden text, choose Hidden Text from the **View** menu.

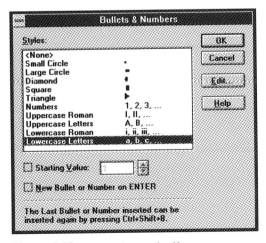

**Figure 3.10**  **Inserting a bullet**

# Mouse Formatting Tricks

· · · · · · · · · · · · · · · · · · · · · · · · · · · · · · · · · · ·

WordPerfect 6.0 comes with several built-in aids to formatting that let you use the mouse instead of choosing from menus. These are the ruler and the various button bars, such as the WordPerfect, Layout, Font, and Tables button bars. You'll see tricks for them in this section.

### Use QuickFormat to Copy Formatting

Before you read any more formatting tips, you should be aware of the most basic formatting trick of all: Once you've formatted something the way you want it, you can *copy that formatting* to other text. You can copy character attributes, such as boldfacing and fonts, as well as paragraph formatting, such as line spacing and indents.

To do this, click in a paragraph that's formatted the way you want it. Then click the QuickFormat button on the WordPerfect button bar. The first time, you'll be asked whether you want to copy character formatting, paragraph formatting, or both; just press **Enter** if you're copying both. The pointer changes shape to a paint-roller icon, and you can drag over text to format it the same way that the original paragraph was formatted. You can do this over and over to more text in different locations in your document. To stop copying formatting, click the Quick-Format button again.

### Specialized Button Bars for Specialized Formatting

WordPerfect 6.0 comes with several predefined button bars, and there are formatting buttons on many of them. The WordPerfect button bar has buttons for indenting text, creating bulleted and numbered lists, and doing a QuickFormat. The Layout button bar has buttons for justifying text as well as setting tabs and creating indents (Figure 3.11). The Font button bar lets you switch text to super- or subscript, shadow, and so forth with the click of a button; and the Tables button bar has specialized buttons for formatting in tables.

To switch to a different button bar, click with the right mouse button on any button bar and then choose the button bar you want.

Here are some suggestions for getting the most out of these button bars:

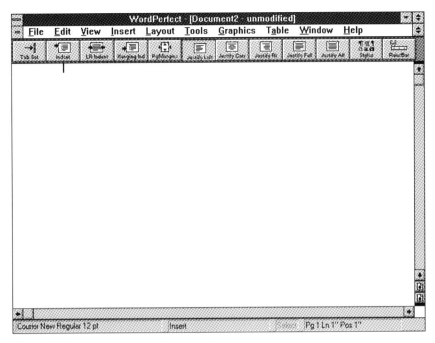

**Figure 3.11** The Layout button bar

♦ If you're changing fonts and sizes in a document or switching to subscript and superscripts, display the Fonts button bar. Save all your font-change work for a time when that button bar is displayed.

♦ For complicated layouts, such as multiple tab settings, columns, and justification changes, display the Layout button bar.

♦ Display the Outline button bar when you're working in outlines.

♦ If you're creating or editing tables, switch to the Table button bar.

♦ Keep the WordPerfect button bar displayed the rest of the time for chores, such as creating bulleted lists, printing envelopes, inserting graphics, and so forth.

See Chapter 4 for lots more tricks you can use to create your own custom button bars for specialized tasks.

### Use the Ruler Bar for Basic Formatting

The ruler bar (Figure 3.12) makes doing basic formatting, such as changing margins and tab stops, much easier and faster, because you don't have to pick from menus or memorize keyboard shortcuts; you just click with the mouse on the ruler settings. In addition, you can see at a glance the settings that are in effect.

To display the ruler, press **Alt+Shift+F3** or choose **R**uler Bar from the **V**iew menu.

### Customize the Ruler Bar

Click with the right mouse button on the ruler bar and choose Preferences. Then, in the dialog box you'll see (Figure 3.13), you can set up the ruler so that it will automatically be displayed in all the documents you open. You can also turn off the invisible grid that tabs "snap to" (about every .06 of an inch), hide the ruler guides, and change how the ruler is displayed.

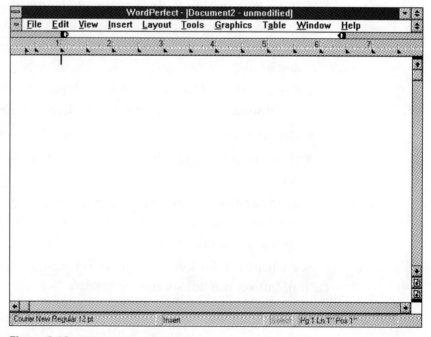

**Figure 3.12** Displaying the ruler

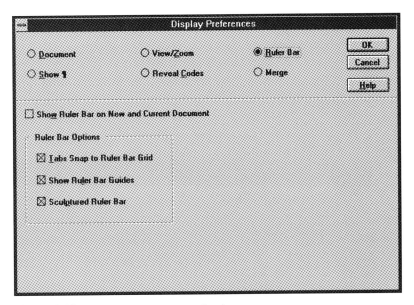

**Figure 3.13** **Setting up your ruler bar**

### *Changing the Ruler Bar's Units of Measurement*

To switch to a different unit of measurement for the ruler, choose Preferences from the File menu, double-click on Display, and click Document. Next to the Status Bar/Ruler display, choose a different unit of measure, such as points or centimeters.

### *Use the Ruler Bar's QuickMenus*

Click with the right mouse button on the ruler bar to display a handy QuickMenu (Figure 3.14) that lets you set all kinds of tabs and hide the ruler bar.

Click with the right mouse button on a margin marker on the ruler bar to get a different QuickMenu (Figure 3.15), one that lets you format paragraphs, change margins, set up columns and tables, and set tabs.

# Margin Tricks

### *Quick Margin Changes*

To change right, left, top, and bottom margins, double-click on a margin marker on the ruler. You'll see the dialog box in Figure 3.16, where

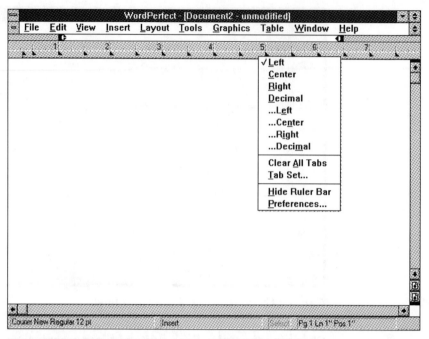

**Figure 3.14**   One of the ruler bar's QuickMenus

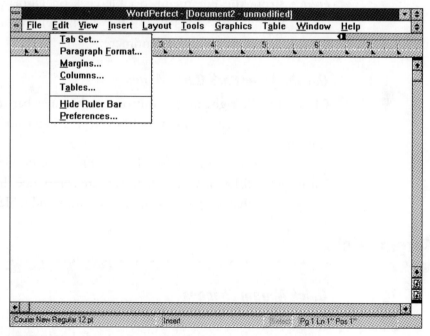

**Figure 3.15**   Another QuickMenu on the ruler bar

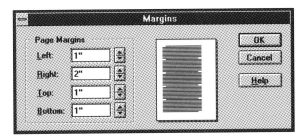

**Figure 3.16** Displaying the Margins dialog box

you can change all sorts of things about the margins, as you'll see in the next tricks.

### Need Text in the Top Margin?

Usually, WordPerfect won't print text in the top margin. Use this slick trick to make it print on the bottom line of the top margin. Choose **T**ypesetting from the Layout menu; then choose **W**ord/Letterspacing; then check the Baseline Placement for Typesetting box (Figure 3.17).

### Need Text Outside the Left Margin?

**Shift+Tab** is the shortcut for Margin Release, which is also called a back tab, and it moves the insertion point to the previous tab setting. If the insertion point is at the left margin, pressing **Shift+Tab** moves it outside the left margin.

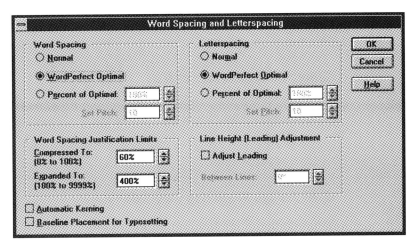

**Figure 3.17** Check Baseline Placement for Typesetting to get text in the top margin.

What's moving out beyond the left margin good for? Well, you might want to number a paragraph or two out in the left margin. To do this, press **Home** to move to the beginning of the line. Then press **Shift+Tab** and type your paragraph number. Press **Tab**; then start typing the paragraph.

If you want WordPerfect to automatically number paragraphs, use the Bullet button on the WordPerfect button bar, as explained in the trick "Instant Bulleted and Numbered Lists" earlier in this chapter.

# Tricks with Tabs and Indents

### Quickly Set a Decimal Tab with Alt+F7

Use this quick slick trick to set a decimal tab when you need to type a few rows of numbers that align on a decimal, like this:

$ 29.98

119.95

9.95

Just press **Alt+F7** and type the number. On the next line, press **Alt+F7** again and type that number. You get the idea.

Use this trick if you're typing only a few numbers that have to align, because you need to press the shortcut combination at the beginning of each line. Use the ruler or the Tab Set dialog box if you're planning to type lots of numbers to align in a column, or to set up a table.

### Setting Different Kinds of Tabs

The trick to setting different types of tabs with the ruler is to right-click on the bottom of the ruler bar. You'll see a QuickMenu (Figure 3.18) that lets you pick which type of tab you want. Then just click on the ruler to set that tab.

### Open the Tab Set Dialog Box Quickly

Use this quick slick trick instead of choosing Line and then Tab Set from the Layout menu. Simply double-click on any tab marker to display the Tab Set dialog box (Figure 3.19).

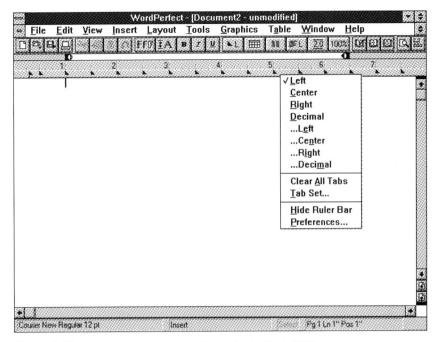

**Figure 3.18** Setting tabs with the ruler's QuickMenu

### *Tricks for Opening the Tab Set Dialog Box*

There are several different slick ways to open the Tab Set dialog box:

♦ Double-click the tab button on the power bar.

♦ Double-click a tab marker on the ruler.

♦ Double-click on a tab code in Reveal Codes.

♦ Click the Tab Set button on the Layout button bar.

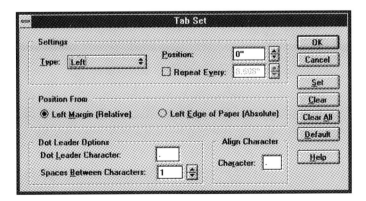

**Figure 3.19** The Tab Set dialog box

♦ Click with the right mouse button on the ruler and choose Tab Set from the QuickMenu.

### Setting Evenly Spaced Tabs

Here's the trick for setting tabs at evenly spaced increments, such as every inch. (Normally, they're set every half inch.)

Double-click on a tab marker to bring up the Tab Set dialog box; then click Clear All. Enter the position where you want the first tab; then click Repeat Every and enter the spacing you want between each tab, such as 1 for one inch.

### Quickly Deleting a Tab or Two

To delete a tab marker, put the cursor on it and then drag it off the ruler. What could be simpler?

### Delete All Tabs before Setting New Ones

Trust me; it's much easier to see what you're doing if you clear all tabs before you try to set new ones. Click that Clear All button in the Tab Set dialog box.

### Change the Size of Indents by Resetting Tabs

WordPerfect uses the tab settings that are in effect to determine the size of indents. So if your indents are larger or smaller than you'd like, reset the tabs. For example, if you want quarter-inch indents instead of half-inch indents (based on the default half-inch tab settings), reset tabs. Use the Tab Set dialog box to reset tabs in equal increments, as you saw in an earlier trick.

### Set a Hard Tab to Use on Only One Line

When you reset tabs, the new tab settings take effect from the *beginning of the paragraph* through the rest of the document. If all you want to do is set tabs to use *on one line* and then go back to the default tab settings after that line, set a hard tab. Here's how to do it. Put the cursor where you want the tab; then choose Line from the Layout menu; then choose **O**ther codes. You'll see the dialog box in Figure 3.20. Pick the kind of tab you want.

**Other Codes**

Hard Tab Codes:
- ○ Left [Hd Left Tab]
- ○ Center [Hd Center Tab]
- ○ Right [Hd Right Tab]
- ○ Decimal [Hd Dec Tab]

Hard Tab Codes with Dot Leaders:
- ○ Left [...Hd Left Tab]
- ○ Center [...Hd Center Tab]
- ○ Right [...Hd Right Tab]
- ○ Decimal [...Hd Dec Tab]

[Insert] [Cancel] [Help]

Hyphenation Codes:
- ○ Hyphen [- Hyphen]
- ○ Hyphen Character
- ○ Soft Hyphen [- Soft Hyphen]
- ○ Hyphenation Soft Return [HyphSRt]
- ○ Cancel Hyphenation of Word [Cancel Hyph]

Other Codes:
- ○ Hard Space [HSpace]
- ○ End Centering/Alignment [END Cntr/Align]
- ○ Thousands Separator [.]

**Figure 3.20** Setting a hard tab

### Use Tables for Complicated Rows and Columns

A good rule of thumb: Anything longer than three columns and three rows should be done as a table instead of using tabs. Really.

### Changing the Alignment Character

You've often seen those memos that start with

Memo to:

From:

Subject:

To get this kind of effect in your documents, all you need to do is change the alignment character from a period to a colon. You can change it to any other character, too, including any WordPerfect character.

To do this, open the Tab Set dialog box and type the character you want to use for text to be aligned on, such as a colon (:), in the Character box under Align Character. To insert a special WordPerfect character, click in that box, press **Ctrl+W**, and double-click on the character you want.

As you're typing, whenever you want text to align on that character, press **Tab** until you get to that tab stop (usually, it's best to delete all the extra tabs that you're not going to be using). Go ahead and type; whenever you type that character, text will align around it.

### Creating Dot Leaders

Here's a slick trick for creating text with dot leaders, which you often see in tables of contents and simple lists like this:

Chapter 1 . . . . . . . . . . . . . . . . . Page   1

Chapter 2 . . . . . . . . . . . . . . . . . Page 44

Just type the flush-left text; then press **Alt+F7** twice and type the text that's supposed to have the dot leaders in front of it.

Use **Shift+F7** twice for centered text with dot leaders.

---

### Always Use the Tab Key to Create Indents

If you indent text by pressing the space bar, it may look OK on the screen, but if you switch to a different font or open the document in another program, your indents will get messed up. That's because a space is a relative measure: It depends on the font you're using and its size. So, create indents by pressing the **Tab** key or one of the indent keyboard shortcuts that you'll see in the next few tricks.

---

### More Tab Shortcuts

When you're ready to use the tabs you've set, use these shortcuts:

| | |
|---|---|
| **Tab** | To indent |
| **F7** | To indent and hang |
| **Ctrl+F7** | For a hanging indent (an "outdent") |
| **Ctrl+Shift+F7** | For a double indent |

### Create a Hanging Indent with Ctrl+F7

Hanging indents are those in which all the lines of a paragraph are indented except for the first line. You'll see these often in lists like bibliographies. Here's an example:

Nelson, Kay Yarborough. *Slick Tricks for WordPerfect 6.*
        New York: Random House, 1994.

Remember from a trick earlier in this chapter that if there's not enough "hang" to your indent, reset the tabs.

### Indenting Text Equally from Right and Left Margins

WordPerfect has a built-in Left/Right Indent shortcut: press **Ctrl+ Shift+F7**. (There's also a LR Indent button on the Layout button bar that does the same thing.) The next text you type will be centered between the right and left margins until you press **Enter**.

To left/right indent a paragraph you've already typed, block it first; then press **Ctrl+Shift+F7** or choose Center alignment for it. This effect is often used for displayed quotations in text.

If your paragraph isn't indented the way you'd like, open a Reveal Codes window and see if there isn't a stray [Tab] at the beginning of the line. Delete it.

### Indenting the First Line of All Paragraphs

Instead of having to remember to press **Tab** each time you start a new paragraph, use WordPerfect 6.0's new First Line Indent feature. Once you turn it on, all your paragraphs will automatically be indented.

Right-click on the ruler and choose Paragraph Format from the QuickMenu to open the Paragraph Format dialog box (Figure 3.21); then enter the amount by which you want text indented in the First Line Indent box. That's it: Your paragraphs will now resemble those in Figure 3.22, indented by whatever amount you specified. Put this code in your initial codes style if you want the same first line indent in all your documents. (See the trick "Use the Initial Style Feature to Create Default Settings" earlier in this chapter for how to do this.)

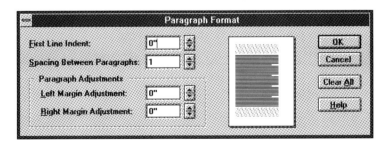

**Figure 3.21**  The Paragraph Format dialog box

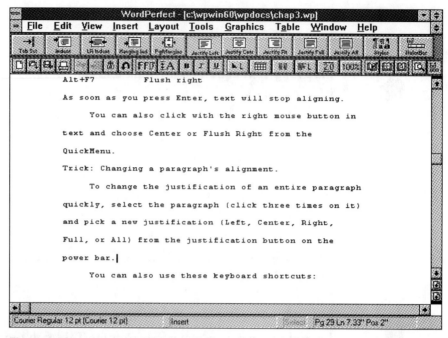

**Figure 3.22**   Indenting the first lines of paragraphs

### *Creating a Flush-and-Hang Indent*

Aligning text flush right after a number is one of the easiest things you can do in WordPerfect, but for some reason it's one thing I get asked about a lot. Just type the number and then press **F7**! Here's an example of what you'll get:

1   The Indent key, F7, instantly creates beautiful flush-and-hang
    indents in which all lines after the first align with the text of the first line.

### *Remove Indents by Deleting Their Codes*

Once you've created an indent, text you type sometimes just won't go where you think it ought to. To remove an indent that isn't working the way you'd like it, open the Reveal Codes window and delete the offending code.

### *Start WordPerfect with Factory Settings*

Use the command **wpwin /x** in the Program Manager's Run box to start WordPerfect with the original factory settings in effect, no matter how you've changed the initial style.

WordPerfect's factory format settings are as follows:

Left justification

Single spacing

No page numbering

Tabs every half inch

One-inch left, right, top, and bottom margins

## Alignment Tricks

### *Aligning Text As You Type*

Use these handy keyboard shortcuts to align a line of text as you type:

**Shift+F7**   Center

**Alt+F7**   Flush right

As soon as you press **Enter**, text will stop aligning.

You can also click with the right mouse button in text and choose Center or Flush Right from the QuickMenu.

### *Changing a Paragraph's Alignment*

To change the justification of an entire paragraph quickly, select the paragraph (click three times on it) and pick a new justification (Left, Center, Right, Full, or All) from the justification button on the power bar.

You can also use these keyboard shortcuts:

**Ctrl+L**   Left justification

**Ctrl+R**   Right justification

**Ctrl+E**   Centered justification

**Ctrl+J**   Full justification

If you're displaying the Layout button bar, you can click the Justification buttons to switch to a different justification.

### Full and All Justifications Cause Unusual Word Spacing

WordPerfect stretches text to fit equally between the left and right margins (Full justification) by adding space between the words. It can add as much as four times the usual amount of space between the words. Sometimes you won't like the results. Likewise, with Justify All, the program will s t r e t c h out short lines, which can be quite ugly.

### Quickly Centering Text in Columns

To center text in columns, put the cursor in the column and choose Center justification from the power bar's justification button menu.

If you want to center a heading (just one line) over a column, put the cursor at the beginning of the heading and press Shift+F7.

### Tabs Prevent Centered Text

If text isn't getting centered between the right and left margins, open the Reveal Codes window (**Alt+F3**) and see if you there aren't invisible [Tab] codes in the line. Take 'em out, and you'll get correctly centered text.

# Line Spacing Tricks

### Changing Line Spacing

To change line spacing quickly, click the line spacing button on the power bar and choose the spacing you want. Choose Other if you want to enter odd spacings, such as 2.75 or 4.25. (Test-print these on your printer to see if it can handle them.)

When you change line spacing, the entire paragraph you're in, as well as the rest of the document, changes, too. If you want to change line spacing in only part of your text, select it first.

### Changing Spacing between Paragraphs

A very sophisticated touch that you can easily add to your documents is changing the amount of space between paragraphs instead of using paragraph indents. To do this, go to the beginning of your document or insert the code in your initial style. (See the trick "Use Initial Style Feature to Create Default Settings" earlier in this chapter.)

To specify spacing between paragraphs, right-click on the ruler and choose Paragraph Format to bring up the Paragraph Format dialog box. In the Spacing Between Paragraphs box, enter a new number. Remember that you can use points here by entering the number followed by the letter **p**.

### Adjust Line Height to Change Line Spacing

Line spacing is determined by the line height. So if you don't like what you're getting for double or single spacing, change the line height. With single spacing, the distance from the baseline of one line of text to the baseline of the next line of text is one line height. With double spacing, there are two line heights between baselines.

Now, the trick is that there are two ways to change line height: first, by using a fixed line height; and second, by changing the leading. If you want to change line height in just part of a document, change the fixed line height—but read the next trick first.

To change fixed line height, block the text you want to change the line spacing in. Choose **L**ine from the **L**ayout menu; then choose **H**eight. Click Fixed and enter a new measurement for line height.

### Adjusting the Leading

Normally the program adds space, called *leading*, between lines of text in proportionally spaced fonts. (Monospaced fonts, like Courier, have leading built into them.)

To adjust the leading that's being used, choose **T**ypesetting from the **L**ayout menu; then choose **W**ord/Letterspacing. Select Adjust Leading (Figure 3.23). Enter the amount you want to add to the line height, or enter a negative number to decrease line height. Enter the amount in points. Fonts are usually measured in points, and it's easier to think of point sizes than inches for fonts. For example, entering **2p** tells Word-Perfect "two points."

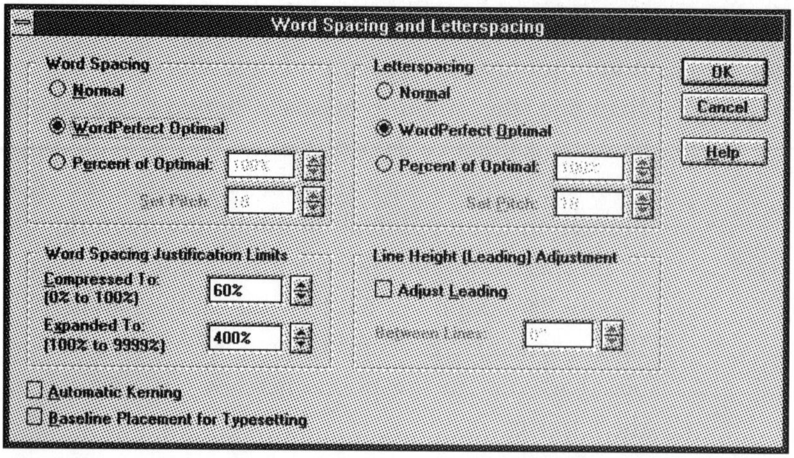

![Word Spacing and Letterspacing dialog box]

**Figure 3.23** The Word Spacing and Letterspacing dialog box

---

## Fixed Line Height Can Cause Trouble

WordPerfect calculates line height automatically so that if you switch to different-sized fonts in a line of text, the line height will change to accommodate the largest font size. If you've chosen a fixed line height that's smaller than your largest font plus a point or two, and then you mix font sizes on a line, some of the tops and bottoms of letters may get chopped off, because WordPerfect isn't automatically compensating for the font size changes. Change the leading to change line height so that WordPerfect will still adjust the line spacing automatically. See the trick "Adjusting the Leading."

### Decrease Line Height for More Text

Sometimes when you're working with columns, you're getting bad column breaks, and no amount of tedious editing will make the last line fit on the page. Try this slick trick: Select a few paragraphs toward the end of your article and decrease the leading in them. Probably nobody will notice, and you'll be able to cram that last line on the page.

# Hyphenation Tricks

### Turn On Hyphenation with Full Justification

When text is justified (spaced evenly between the right and left margins), WordPerfect tries to fill out a line to align equally on both margins. Sometimes you wind up with a   lot   of   spacing   between words. If you turn on hyphenation, this problem will clear up, because the program can then break words at the ends of lines.

To turn on hyphenation, choose Line from the Layout menu; then choose Hyphenation. This starts hyphenation at the beginning of the current paragraph. Go to the beginning of the document to turn it on if you want hyphenation on in the whole document, or use it in your initial style.

---

### If You Turn On Columns, Turn Off Hyphenation

Trust me. Most of the time, if you use hyphenation in narrow text columns, you'll get too many hyphens at the ends of lines. You can turn it back on again after the table or columns.

---

### Turn On Hyphenation after *Writing a Document*

It's easier to let WordPerfect hyphenate a document after you've typed it so that you won't be interrupted for word breaks as you write. Press **Ctrl+Home** to go to the beginning of the document; turn on hyphenation; then move to the end of the document with **Ctrl+End**.

### Instead of Turning On Hyphenation, Insert Hyphens Manually

Most of the time, unless you're using Full justification, you won't want to fool with hyphenation. Thankfully, the program lets you insert all sorts of different kinds of hyphens where you need them: *soft hyphens, hard hyphens*, and *em* and *en dashes* are the only ones you'll usually ever use.

### Soft Hyphen for a Better Line Break

Soft hyphens will appear only when a word is broken at the end of a line. WordPerfect normally inserts soft hyphens automatically, and then only when you've turned hyphenation on. The only time you might want to put in a soft hyphen yourself is when you're not using automatic hyphenation and you want to hyphenate a word for a better line break. If you later edit the document so that the line doesn't break there, the soft hyphen will disappear.

You don't see a soft hyphen on the screen. To get a soft hyphen, press **Ctrl+Shift** and type a hyphen.

### Stop a Hyphenated Word from Being Broken

If you want a word like *commander-in-chief* to be hyphenated, type it just the way it looks, with the hyphens. If you want to make sure that it won't be broken if it occurs at the end of a line (so that commander-in-chief always stays together as one word, for example), use hard hyphens.

To get a hard hyphen, press **Ctrl** and then type the hyphen. Obviously, a hard hyphen wasn't used on the line above.

### Removing Hyphenation

Sometimes even after you've turned off hyphenation, hyphens appear in your text. These are either hyphens you've put there manually (and you probably want to leave those alone, because they're there for a reason) or they're hyphens WordPerfect inserted when it prompted you about whether you wanted it to hyphenate a word or tell it exactly where you wanted the hyphen to go. WordPerfect won't delete those hyphens when you turn off hyphenation.

To strip all those pesky, unwanted hyphens out of your document, go to the beginning of the document (**Ctrl+Home**). Then press **Ctrl+F2** and choose Codes from the Match menu. Double-click on -Soft Hyphen (Figure 3.24). Make sure the Replace With box is empty; then press **Enter**.

### Hard Spaces Keep Words on the Same Line

OK, this isn't a hyphenation tip, but it's closely related to the preceding trick. If you don't want a certain phrase to be broken at the end of a line, put hard spaces between the words. To get a hard space, press **Ctrl** and then the space bar.

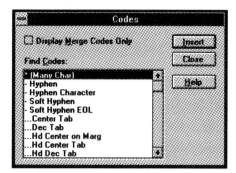

**Figure 3.24** Hyphen codes

For example, say that you have the date September 2, 1994 at the end of a line. If the line breaks anywhere in that date, you may get a stray "1994" on the next line, or the next line may start "2, 1994." Do this with names, too (e.g., "Harry S. Truman"), so that "Harry" won't end one line and "S. Truman" begin the next.

### Em and En Dashes instead of Hyphens

En dashes are longer than hyphens and are often used as minus signs, but strictly speaking, they should be used to indicate ranges of numbers, as in "pages 11–12" or "in the period 1960–62."

Em dashes are longer than en dashes—like this one; they're also called long dashes. Look back at Table 3.1 to see their shortcuts.

If you use em and en dashes a lot, record a macro for each one. Then make a button for them if you'd rather point-and-click to insert them.

# Page Formatting

• • • • • • • • • • • • • • • • • • • • • • • • • • • • • • • • • • •

If you're doing page formatting, display the Page button bar (Figure 3.25). It's got lots of handy buttons for common page-formatting jobs.

### Force a Page Break with Ctrl+Enter

This is a very easy trick, but if you don't know it, you can spend hours looking for it on page 456 of the WordPerfect 6.0 manual. So, here it is: To force a page break (create a hard page break), press **Ctrl+Enter**. You'll see a double line on the screen (Figure 3.26) indicating where the page breaks.

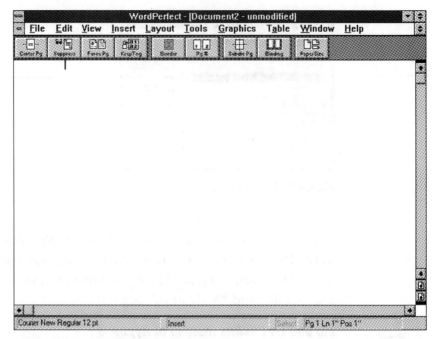

**Figure 3.25** The Page button bar

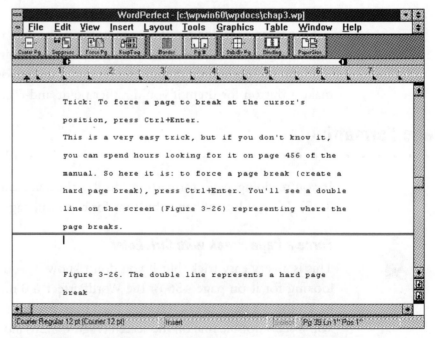

**Figure 3.26** The double line represents a hard page break

Now, the opposite trick: To delete a hard page break, put the cursor just below the line that represents the page break; then press **Backspace** or **Del**.

You can also locate the [HPg] code that represents the hard page break and delete it. That will delete the page break, too.

### Keeping Headings with Their Text

While we're on the subject of page breaks . . . To keep a heading with the text that follows it so that the heading doesn't appear by itself at the bottom of a page, use a little-known feature called Conditional End of Page.

Put the cursor in the heading; then count down to the last line that you want to keep with the heading. If you're using double spacing, each line counts as two lines. Then click the KeepTog button on the Page button bar, or choose **P**age from the **L**ayout menu, choose **K**eep Text Together, and enter that number as the number of lines to keep together (Figure 3.27).

### Avoid Stray Lines with Widow/Orphan Protect

To prevent single lines of paragraphs being printed at the tops or bottoms of pages, check the Widow/Orphan box in the Keep Text Together dialog box.

### Avoid Breaking Tables and Charts with Block Protect

To keep a table or list from being split between two pages, use the Block Protect feature. As long as the table consists of one page or less, it will

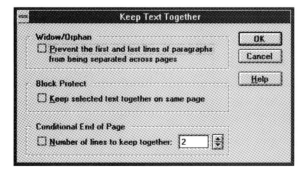

**Figure 3.27** Protecting against unwanted page breaks

be kept on one page. To use this feature, select the whole table, list, chart, or whatever, and then check the Block Protect box in the Keep Text Together dialog box.

### Centering Text on a Page

WordPerfect can automatically center all the text on a page for you so that you don't have to figure out how many blank lines go above and below the text.

Click the Center Pg button on the Page button bar, or choose **Page** from the Layout menu; then choose **Center**. In the dialog box, choose **Center Current Page** (to center the text on the page you're on) or Center **Pages** (to center the current page and all the pages after it).

This will center the text vertically on the page. If you want the text centered both vertically *and* horizontally, as in a cover sheet, use Center justification on it, too.

### Putting a Border around a Page

WordPerfect will insert a border around a page as well as around a paragraph, as you saw in an earlier trick. Click the Border button on the Page button bar and pick a border style (Figure 3.28). This is a nice touch for cover sheets.

### Numbering Pages

WordPerfect doesn't number pages unless you tell it to. Click the Pg # button on the Page button bar and choose a position for the page number (Figure 3.29).

Since the program is preset not to number pages, you have to remember to turn on page numbering in each document whose pages you want numbered. This can be a pain. Put the code for page numbering in your initial style if you want numbered pages in all your documents.

If you don't want all your documents to have page numbers, record a macro that will turn on page numbering in the style you want; then assign it to a button so that you can just click on it to turn on page numbering at the beginning of any document you want.

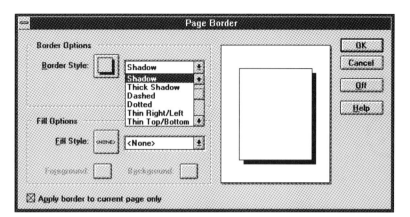

**Figure 3.28**   Choosing a page border

### *Changing the Font for Page Numbers*

If you don't do anything else, WordPerfect will use the same font and size for page numbers that it uses for the body of your document. Sometimes it's nicer to use a different font, or at least a smaller one, for page numbers. Click the Font button in the Page Numbering dialog box. Then pick another font or size, or switch to italics or boldface—whatever you like. Put this code in your initial style if you want to make it permanent for all your documents.

### *Including Text with Page Numbers*

If you want pages to be numbered and include text with them, such as "Chapter" or "section," click the Options button in the Page Numbering dialog box. Then type the text you want, leaving the [Pg #] as a

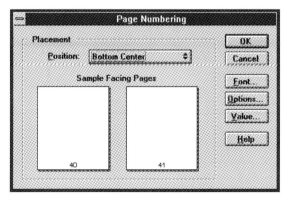

**Figure 3.29**   Picking a page number position

placeholder for the actual page number. See Figure 3.30 for an example of how to create page number text, such as "Annual Report, page 5."

---

**Be Careful Using Fancy Page Numbering**

If you're going to generate a table of contents or an index, don't use text with your page numbers, or you'll get things like "Chapter 4, Page 45" in your tables of contents.

---

### Starting Page Numbering with a Specific Number

To force WordPerfect to use a number you specify as a starting page number, click the Value button in the Page Numbering dialog box and enter the page number you want to start with in the Numbering Value dialog box (Figure 3.31). This is the quick and easy way to number pages in separate chapters consecutively if you're not using the Master Document feature.

### Forcing a Page to Be Odd or Even

When you're printing a document on both sides of the paper or preparing one that's going to be printed and bound, you'll want new chapters

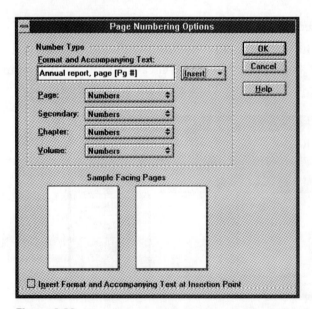

**Figure 3.30**   You can include text with page numbers

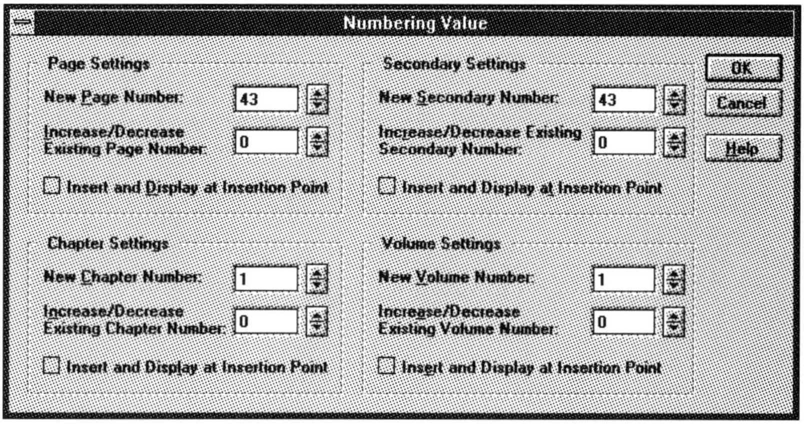

**Figure 3.31** Forcing a page number

or sections to start on right-hand (odd-numbered) pages. WordPerfect can take care of this for you if you tell it to. Click the Force Pg button on the Page button bar. Then choose **O**dd to force a new right-hand page or **E**ven to force a left-hand page. WordPerfect will add a hard page break, or even a blank page, if it's needed.

# Header and Footer Tricks

In WordPerfect, headers and footers can contain all kinds of things besides text: page numbers, the date, cross references to other pages—even graphics. You can have a different header and footer on each page and even alternate headers or footers on odd (right-hand) and even (left-hand) pages. You can even have a special kind of header/footer called a watermark, that appears on all the pages of a document, not necessarily at the top or bottom of the page, but wherever you specify.

### *Create Headers, Footers, and Watermarks*

To create a header (or footer or watermark), switch to Page view if you're not already there. Right-click in the header or footer part of the page (the top or bottom of the page) and choose Header/Footer or Watermark from the QuickMenu. You can also choose **H**eader/Footer or **W**atermark from the **L**ayout menu. Then choose Header or Footer A or B (you can have two of each) and click Create. You'll see a dialog box (Figure 3.32) where you can type the text for the header or footer.

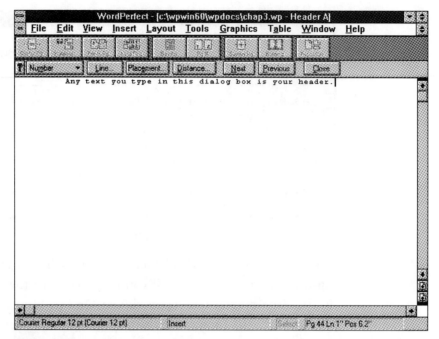

**Figure 3.32**   Creating a header

### *Getting Page Numbers in Headers and Footers*

If you want a header or footer to display the current page, when you get to the part of the text where the page number should appear, click Number in the Header/Footer feature bar and choose **P**age Number.

For example, to create text for a header or footer that says "Chapter 5, page *n*," where *n* is the current page number, you'd type Chapter 5, page and then click Number and Page Number.

### *Easy Header/Footer Editing*

Switch to Page mode; then you can double-click on a header or footer (or watermark) to edit it. Click with the *right* mouse button to display the QuickMenu for headers and footers (Figure 3.33).

### *Creating a Watermark*

Easy. Play the WATERMARK macro that comes with WordPerfect. You won't have to bother with learning how to do it, and you can choose from several different graphic images, or use text that you specify. Just press **Alt+F10**, enter watermark, and press **Enter**. You'll be prompted

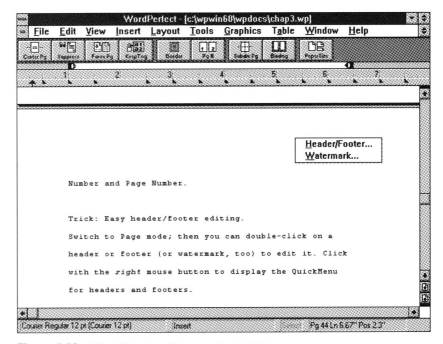

**Figure 3.33** The Header/Footer QuickMenu

for what to do next. It will create a watermark from text that you type or from a list of graphic images.

### Creating a "Page n of n" Footer

This is a handy footer (or header) to use in a long document, where you want to show how many total pages there are as well as the number of the page you're on.

Creating one of these is fairly complicated, because it makes you use WordPerfect's cross-reference feature. But there's a slick way: Use the PAGEXOFY macro that comes with the program. Choose **P**lay from the **M**acro menu or press **Alt+F10**; then enter **pagexofy** and press **Enter**. Switch to Page view to see its effects.

### Including the Date in a Header or Footer

To include the date in a header or footer, press **Ctrl+D** to insert the text of today's date, or **Ctrl+Shift+F5** to insert a date code. If you insert the date as text, it remains that day's date; if you insert it as a code, the date is updated whenever you open the document.

## Don't Use Page Numbering and Headers or Footers

If you turn on page numbering and set up a header or footer in the same place, text may overlap when your document is printed. You can get around this by putting page numbers in the header or footer, as you saw in the previous tip. Or you can add a hard return as the *first* line in the header or as the *last* line in the footer so that the page number will print on a line by itself.

### Apply Formatting in Headers and Footers

Don't forget that any time you're creating a header or footer, you can use WordPerfect's regular formatting commands for font changes, italics and boldface, special characters, margin changes, centering, flush right, and so forth. It's easy to create headers and footers with multiple elements like this one:

*Kay Yarborough Nelson • 5751 Pescadero Creek Road • Pescadero, CA 94060*

### Viewing Headers and Footers

Use Page view, because headers and footers don't show up in Draft view. If you're alternating headers and footers on different pages, use Two-Page view, because you can see both pages at once.

### Multiple Headers or Footers in a Document

Remember, you can have two headers and two footers on any given double-page spread. Header (Footer) A is for left-hand pages and Header (Footer) B is for right-hand pages. You can also alternate two different headers or footers between odd and even pages, so you could have one header displaying the chapter number and name on even (left-hand) pages and the date on odd (right-hand) pages. If you alternate between odd and even pages, it's a nice touch to have text flush right on odd pages so that your header or footer text appears flush left on even pages and flush right on odd pages.

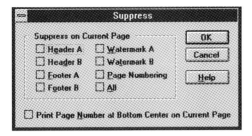

**Figure 3.34** Suppressing headers and footers

### Turning Off Headers and Footers on a Page

Sometimes you may have a page with artwork or a big table on it, and you don't want headers or footers to be printed on that page. You can suppress them for that page. Just click the Suppress button on the Page button bar. Then, in the dialog box that you'll see (Figure 3.34), choose what you want to suppress.

Another good use for this trick is to set up a footer for business letters and then immediately suppress it on the first page of the letter so that it'll appear on the second and subsequent pages only.

### Adjust Spacing Below Headers and above Footers

With the cursor on the page where you want to adjust the spacing around the header or footer, choose Header/Footer from the Layout menu and then choose Create or Edit, depending on whether you've already set up the header or footer. Then click the Distance button and enter a new spacing (Figure 3.35).

### Centering a Watermark on the Page

If you've ever wondered how to get a watermark where you wanted it, here's the secret: Press **Enter** until it's in the middle of the page; then use Center justification on it.

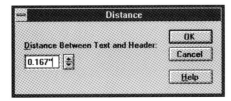

**Figure 3.35** Adjusting the space around headers/footers

If you're inserting a figure as a watermark, don't worry about it. WordPerfect will automatically center it on the page for you.

# Using Columns

WordPerfect 6.0 lets you create two different types of columns: newspaper columns and parallel columns. With newspaper columns, text flows from the bottom of one column to the top of the next. With parallel columns, text stays adjacent to the entries on either side of them.

### Don't Use Parallel Columns

Remember this basic slick trick: Don't use parallel columns at all. They're a major nuisance to create and edit. It's much easier to type text in table cells than to set up and use parallel columns. It's a lot easier to format, too, once the text is typed. If you don't want any rules around cells, don't use rules in your table.

Also, forget about setting up tables with tabs unless you're creating a maximum of three entries, no more. Make a table instead. Columns of tabbed data are notoriously difficult to edit in WordPerfect. Tables are easy, so use them.

### In Newspaper Columns, Type Text First

Turning typed text into columns is much more efficient than typing text in columns. For one thing, having a large number of columns displayed on the screen can slow down your system, especially if you're using lots of graphics and making font changes. Type text first; then format it into columns. Just click on the Column button on the power bar to convert text to up to five newspaper columns. Use the **C**olumns command on the **L**ayout menu and choose **D**efine if you want more than five columns or if you want parallel columns.

You can convert text to either parallel or newspaper columns, but it's usually easier with newspaper columns. If you convert text to parallel columns, you'll need to go through it and press **Ctrl+Enter** at each point where you want a column break.

### WordPerfect Adjusts Newspaper Columns on the Page

WordPerfect can automatically balance newspaper columns so that they're equal in length and fill a page. Let it! Although you can cheat and add a line or two of blank space or create a hard page break with **Ctrl+Enter**, let the program do the hard work. Check Balanced Newspaper under Type in the Columns dialog box (Figure 3.36).

### Use Parallel Columns with Block Protect

I've already told you why you shouldn't use parallel columns, but if you really want to, by all means choose Parallel Columns with Block Protect, instead of plain old Parallel Columns. That way, if a line in one column has to be broken between two pages, the whole column will move to the next page. This looks much nicer in most cases than breaking a column in the middle, but use Page view to see the effects.

### Ctrl+Enter Breaks Columns

Whenever you want to end one column and start a new one, press **Ctrl+Enter**, just like creating a page break. The column will break at that point and a new one will start.

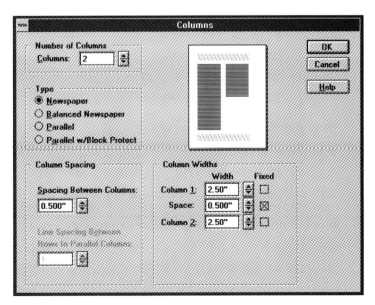

**Figure 3.36** The Columns dialog box

### Changing Columns Back to Text

To eliminate columns, the safest way is to locate the [Col Def] code that's at the beginning of the columns and delete it. If you simply choose Columns Off from the pop-up menu that appears when you click on the Columns button, and the cursor isn't at the exact start of the columns, only the text from the cursor's point on is changed.

### Shortcuts for Moving through Columns

If you're editing text in columns, you'll usually find that it's easiest to use a mouse, because you can just click on the spot you want to edit. There are built-in keyboard shortcuts for moving through columns, though, and here are a few of them:

**Alt+Right arrow** and **Alt+Left arrow** move one column to the right or left.

**Ctrl+Home+Up arrow** and **Ctrl+Home+Down arrow** move to the top or bottom of the column you're in.

Press **Ctrl+G** and use the Go To dialog box to move between columns.

### Edit Columns with the Mouse

The easiest way to adjust text in columns is to display the ruler bar and use the mouse. To change the column widths, just drag a column marker (Figure 3.37). To change the gutter (the space between columns), drag it, too. To adjust the right or left margins or change the first-line indent, drag those markers. You'll see ruler guides as you drag to help you position the columns.

### Drag and Drop to Edit Text in Columns

If you're rearranging paragraphs in columns, try using WordPerfect's drag-and-drop feature. The program will reformat the columns for you, and it's often faster than cutting and pasting.

### Mix Different Numbers of Columns on Same Page

With WordPerfect 6.0, it's easy. (With another popular word-processing program whose name I won't mention, it's not.) Just define as many columns as you want, move to the end of that text, and define the next set of columns you want, or turn off columns to return to one-column text.

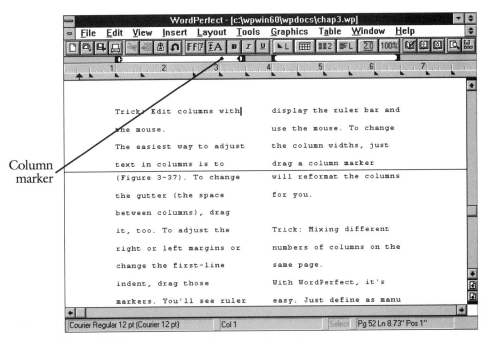

Column marker

**Figure 3.37** Column markers on the ruler

### *Converting Columns to Tables*

If you've laboriously started setting up parallel columns and then decide to take my advice and use a table instead, here's how to convert your completed work to a table. Select the material you've put in parallel columns; then press **F12** (or choose **C**reate from the **T**able menu). Click Parallel Columns and OK. That's it!

### *Vertical Lines between Columns*

Putting vertical lines between columns (Figure 3.38) can lend a sophisticated touch to your documents. To get this effect, put the cursor at the beginning of the first column, but inside the column (make sure the status line displays "Col"); then choose **C**olumns from the **L**ayout menu; then choose **B**order/Fill. In the Column Border dialog box, choose Column Between as the border style. Watch the preview box to see the effects.

You can have lines on all four sides of a column and use a textured background for the column, too. Just make your choices from the Border Style and Fill Style lists.

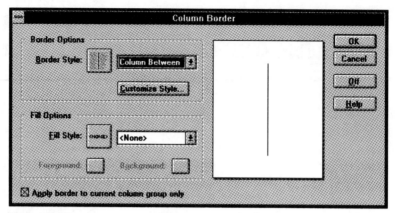

**Figure 3.38** Getting a rule between columns

# Using Styles for Formatting

One of the slickest formatting tricks of all is to use styles for formatting your documents. A *style* is basically just a combination of formatting codes that you can apply to text without having to type all the commands for the codes one by one. Once you've set up a style, you can use it again and again. Styles are complicated to understand but easy to use. If you've never used them before, you can get started by simply using the built-in styles that come with WordPerfect 6.0.

### WordPerfect's Built-In Styles

WordPerfect comes with quite a few built-in styles. To see them, choose **S**tyles from the **L**ayout menu, click the Styles button in the WordPerfect button bar, or press **Alt+F8**. You'll see the Style List dialog box (Figure 3.39). Just double-click on a style in that list, and the current paragraph will be formatted in that style.

Highlight a style and click Edit to see the codes it creates. For example, heading 1 normally creates bold, very large type and marks that paragraph as an entry for a table of contents (Figure 3.40).

### Creating a Style from a Paragraph

The next easiest thing you can do, aside from applying a built-in style, is to create a style from a paragraph you've already formatted. This is a great slick trick for setting up a style quickly from text you've already struggled to format the way you want it:

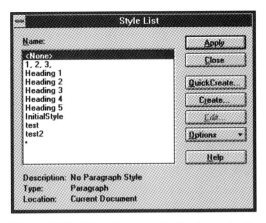

**Figure 3.39** Viewing the built-in style list

1. Put the cursor in the paragraph whose formatting you want to make into a style.
2. Click the Styles button on the WordPerfect button bar.
3. Click QuickCreate.
4. Enter a name and description for your style and click OK. That's it!

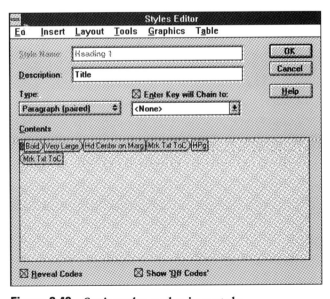

**Figure 3.40** Seeing the codes in a style

## WordPerfect's Style System

You may need a few guideposts to get you through the vocabulary of styles. WordPerfect uses several types of styles:

- Document (Open) styles are turned on at the start of a document and then aren't usually turned off again. These include styles for margins, tabs, page numbering, and so forth.

- Paragraph (Paired) styles apply to entire paragraphs, and you don't have to select a paragraph first to apply the style; Word-Perfect knows which paragraph the cursor is in (if you've used WordPerfect before, you'll be amazed that it does actually know what a paragraph is now!). For this reason, it's usually faster to type a paragraph first and then apply a style to it. You can use paragraph style for headings as well as paragraphs.

- Character (Paired) styles apply, as you might think, to straight text. You can either apply character styles as you type or go back and apply them later; either way is equally efficient.

Paragraph and character styles are paired styles, as opposed to open styles, which means that when they're turned off, the document reverts back to its original formatting.

Wait; there's one more! *System styles* are new in WordPerfect 6.0. Basically, you can think of them as the program's default settings. They affect the format settings of figure captions, footnote numbers, and so forth. These styles are applied any time you use a figure caption, note number, graphics box, or whatever. You can edit these styles, too.

When should you use styles and when should you use macros? Think of it this way: You can apply new formatting to *all* the, say, level 1 headings in a document just by editing the style. With a macro, you'll have to locate each level-1 heading and run the macro on it to change its formatting. Use macros to automate repetitive tasks. Use styles for formatting chores.

### *Enter Key Turns On/Off Paragraph Style*

Usually what you want to do when you press Enter is insert a hard return to begin a new paragraph or create a blank line. But notice that Enter Key will Chain to box in the Styles Editor dialog box (Figure 3.41).

If it reads <Same Style>, each time you press **Enter**, you'll continue to be in the same style. Choose <None>, and then pressing **Enter** turns off the style when you get to the end of the paragraph. This is a useful trick to use for a style that you apply to short paragraphs, such as headings.

The final slick step: Add a hard return [HRt] code to the end of your style so that you don't have to press the **Enter** key twice at the end of a paragraph—once to turn off the style and the other to insert the hard return.

### *Turning Off a Style Quickly*

When you want to turn off a style, use any of these slick tricks:

♦ Press the **Right arrow** key to move past the final style code as you're typing. This trick works on paired styles but not on open styles.

♦ Click the Styles button or press **Alt+F8**, highlight <None>, and press **Enter**.

### *New Styles Override Existing Styles*

Be aware that applying styles isn't cumulative: When you apply a new one, it replaces the old one. Just so you know.

### *Resetting Initial Style to Default Settings*

If you ever want to get your initial style back to WordPerfect's factory settings, use this slick trick. Choose Initial Style from the Style List dialog box and click Options. Choose Reset. You'll be asked "Reset to default state?" Choose Yes, and you've reset the initial style for the document back to the original factory settings.

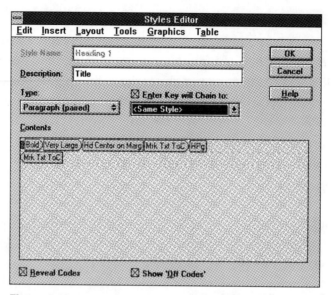

**Figure 3.41** Chaining a style to itself

## Save Styles You Create to Use in Another Document

If you don't save any new styles you create as part of a style library file, you'll have to define them all over again the next time you want to use them in another document. It's easy to save them as a style library file. Just display the Style List dialog box; then choose Options and Setup. Make sure Current Document is checked and choose OK. Then click Options and choose Save As. Type a name for the style library file. Use a name that helps you remember what the styles are for, such as NEWSLTTR.STY. Be sure to end the name with a .STY extension so that you and WordPerfect know it's a style library. Choose which styles you want to save—both yours (User Styles) and WordPerfect's (System Styles) is a safe choice.

Now, all you have to do to use that set of styles again in another document is go to the Style List dialog box, choose Options and Retrieve, and enter the name of the style library you just created.

### *Use Styles Created in WordPerfect 5.1*

You can't use WordPerfect 5.1 style libraries in WordPerfect 6.0, but there's a slick trick you can use to convert them to 6.0 format. Open the 5.1 style library in WordPerfect 6.0, just as though it were a document. You'll see a blank document window, but your 5.1 styles will be listed in the Style List dialog box. Now just save that document as a style library, and you've converted those styles to 6.0 format.

## Tricks with Tables

WordPerfect makes creating rows and columns of text and data really easy, once you understand a few basic slick tricks about tables. With the basic tricks mastered, you can go on to some really slick stuff, like making calculations in a table just as you'd do in a spreadsheet. You can even create fill-in forms with tables.

Don't fool with setting up text columns or tables with tabs unless you're doing a really simple chart or list. Text columns and columns of tabbed data are notoriously difficult to edit in WordPerfect. So why use them when there's an easier way of accomplishing the same thing? Use tables.

### *Table Quick Create Button Creates Tables*

You can also use the shortcut key **F12**, but usually it's faster to simply click the Table Quick Create button and then drag to choose how many rows and columns you want.

---

### *Deleting a Table*

Sometimes you can't delete a table: You press the **Del** or **Backspace** key while the cursor's inside the table, but nothing happens. Use this slick trick to delete a table: Triple-click anywhere inside the table to select it; then press **Del** and choose Entire Table.

You can also open the Reveal Codes window, put the cursor on the [Table Def:] code, and press **Del**. The table will be deleted. If you change your mind and want the table back, press **Ctrl+Z** (Undo).

### Move between Cells in a Table with Tab

You can use the keyboard to move between cells, and this is often faster than clicking with the mouse if you're entering data in side-by-side cells. Press **Tab** to go from cell to cell to the right, or **Shift+Tab** to go backward (to the left). Press **Alt+Down** or **Up arrow** to go up or down one cell.

Here are a couple more:

**Home Home** takes you to the first cell in the row you're in.

**End End** takes you to the last cell in the row you're in.

### Ctrl+Tab Puts a Tab in a Table

Normally, when you press the **Tab** key in a table, you simply move to the next cell to the right. But sometimes you'll want to format text by inserting a tab. To put a tab in a table, press **Ctrl+Tab**.

### Fancy Tabs and Tabs with Dot Leaders

While we're on the subject of tabs, here's how to put all kinds of tabs and indents in tables:

| | |
|---|---|
| Left tab | **Ctrl+Tab** |
| Right tab | **Alt+F7** |
| Center tab | **Shift+F7** |
| Indent | **F7** |
| Double indent | **Ctrl+Shift+F7** |
| Hanging indent | **Ctrl+F7** |

To set a tab with a dot leader, press the shortcut key twice. For example, **Al+F7 Alt+F7** sets a right-aligned dot-leader tab.

### Selecting in Tables

Use these handy shortcuts for selecting in tables:

♦ To select a row or single cell, move the cursor to the side of a cell until it changes to an arrow. Then click once to select the cell, or twice to select the row.

♦ To select a column, move the cursor to the top or bottom of a cell. When you see the arrow, click to select the cell or double-click to select the column.

♦ To select the whole table, triple-click whenever you see the arrow cursor (move it to any side of a cell).

You can also drag over cells to select them, and that's often faster than any keyboard shortcut.

### *Changing Column Widths Quickly*

To change a column's width, move the cursor to the line separating the column you want to change. It will become a two-headed crosshair. Drag the column line to the new position where you want it.

If you're displaying the ruler bar, you can drag the downward-pointing arrowhead that represents the column marker, too (see Figure 3.42).

### *Shortcuts for Inserting Rows and Columns*

Use these handy shortcuts for inserting a single row:

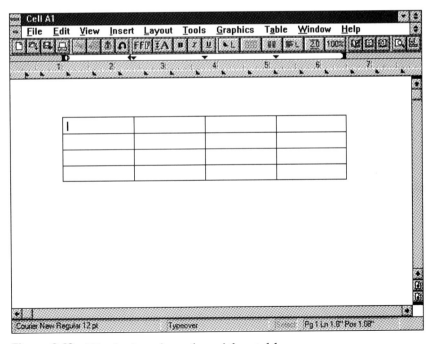

**Figure 3.42**  **Displaying the ruler with a table**

♦ To insert a row above the cursor, press **Alt+Ins**.

♦ To insert a row below the cursor, press **Alt+Shift+Ins**.

♦ To add a row to the end of the table, press **Tab** when the cursor is in the last cell of the table.

### Deleting Columns and Rows Quickly

Select the rows or columns you want to delete. Right-click and choose Del from the Tables QuickMenu (Figure 3.43) or just press **Del**, choose Columns or Rows, and press **Enter**.

If you didn't select the rows or columns first, enter the number of them you want to delete.

Choose Cell Contents to delete just the text, leaving the cells.

### Restoring Table Text

If you delete a cell's contents and need to get them back, press **Ctrl+Z** (if deleting was the last thing you did) or **Esc** (to get the last three deletions back). A simple trick, but handy if you've deleted a string of complicated numbers.

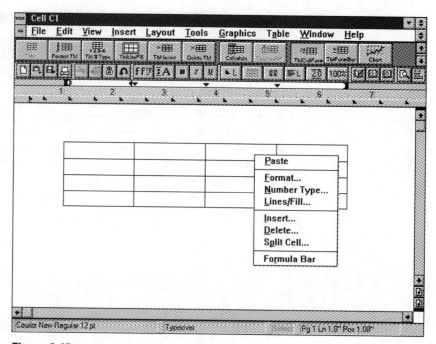

**Figure 3.43**  **Using the Tables QuickMenu**

### Drag-and-Drop to Move or Copy Text in a Table

You can drag-and-drop to move text around in a table. It's often easier than cutting and pasting. Create the new cells you want to put the text in; then drag the text over.

### Paste What You Cut or Copied Again

This is a hidden slick trick. Whatever you cut or copy stays in a buffer until you cut or copy again. So, if you need to copy or paste the same row or column several times, do it once; then move the insertion point to where you want another copy and paste it again.

### Splitting Cells

Haven't you wondered how to get effects like the ones shown in Figure 3.44, where cells are varying sizes and there are unequal numbers of cells in the rows? The trick is to split and join cells to get them that way. Here's how to do it.

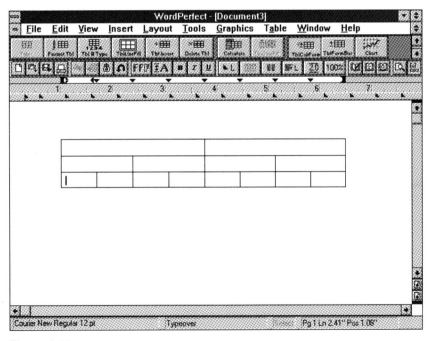

**Figure 3.44** Table with split and joined cells

Put the cursor in the cell you want to split (you can split it into more than two other cells). Right-click and choose Split Cell; then choose **C**olumns or **R**ows and enter how many you want to split it into (Figure 3.45).

### Joining Cells

You can join several cells into one large one. This is a slick trick for getting headings to span several columns in tables. Just select the cells you want to join, right-click, and choose Join Cells. The trick is to select the cells first.

### Text in Joined Cells Will Be Separated by Tabs

WordPerfect doesn't delete text that's already entered in cells that you join. Instead, it separates each entry with a hard tab. You can delete what you don't want, or reformat it.

### You Can Join Tables, Too

If you've got two tables that you want to make into one, don't bother adding rows and columns to one and copying the text from the second into the first. Just join the tables.

The first trick is that the two tables have to have the same number of columns. (Add a couple of blank columns if you need to; you can edit the tables later.) The second trick is that the tables have to be next to each other, with no text or blank lines in between. Open the Reveal Codes window (**Alt+F3**) and make sure that the first table's [ Tbl Off ] code is right next to the second table's [ Tbl Def ] code, and that there aren't any [HRt] codes in between these two codes. Then put the cursor in the first table, right-click, choose **J**oin from the **T**able menu, and then choose Table.

The second table will be formatted like the first table.

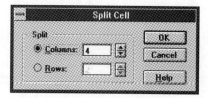

**Figure 3.45**  Splitting cells

### You Can Even Split Tables

If a table is getting too big, or if you suddenly decide you need to add more categories to it, you can split it into two tables. Put the cursor in the row below where you want the table to split, right-click, choose **S**plit from the **T**able menu, and then choose **T**able.

You may need to do a little formatting after you split a table, such as pressing **Enter** to put a few blank lines between the two tables, changing the headings in the second table, and so forth.

If you want to split a table so that it's simply *printed* on two pages, see the trick "Putting a Page Break in a Table" later in the chapter. Split a table the way *this* trick describes only when you want to make it into two separate tables.

### Keep Tables from Splitting between Pages

To keep a table from being broken between pages, if it's less than one page long but just happens to fall low enough on the page that Word-Perfect can't get it all on that page, use the Block Protect feature. Select the table and then choose **P**age from the **L**ayout menu; then choose **K**eep Text Together.

### Putting a Page Break in a Table

To force a page break in a table, put the insertion point where you want the table to break and then press **Ctrl+Enter**.

### Repeating Column Headings on Multipage Tables

If a table's too big to fit on one page, WordPerfect will split it between rows and move part of it to the next page. It won't repeat the column headings unless you tell it to, though. You can have it repeat column headings automatically without retyping the column headings on the second page of the table. If you want to repeat the column headings on the second page of a table, put the cursor in that row. Then right-click, choose Format, and click Row. Finally, in the dialog box that you'll see (Figure 3.46), click the Header Row box.

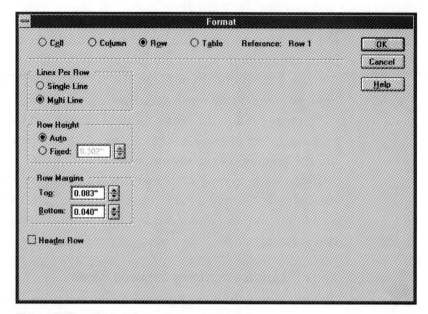

**Figure 3.46**   The Row Format dialog box

### Get a Uniform Table with a Fixed Row Height

Normally, the height of a row will adjust to fit the text that you type in the cells, so if one cell has more text in it than another, the row will expand to accommodate the largest cell. You can turn off this feature so that all the rows in a table will be an equal size. In the Format Row dialog box, choose Fixed and enter the fixed row height you want to use.

### Instantly Creating a Header Row

Well, maybe not "instantly," but faster than you'd do it alone. Play the Heading macro that comes with WordPerfect. It lets you pick a text color and fill pattern or create a header row. Just press **Alt+F10**, enter heading, and press **Enter**.

### Entering a Big Table of Numbers? Check Single Lines of Text.

You can also turn off the feature that allows you to enter more than one line of text in a cell. Click Single Line in the Format Row dialog box, and from then on, each time you press the **Enter** key you'll move to the next cell. This is a handy tip for entering numbers in tables.

### Set Equal Column Widths with the Format Columns Dialog Box

Normally, a column will expand as you type text in it. If this isn't what you want, specify an exact column width and click **F**ixed width in the Format Columns dialog box (Figure 3.47). Right-click in a table, choose Format, and click Column to see it.

### Setting Formats for Several Different Text Appearances

You can format individual cells or blocks of cells outside the table editing window to have different text attributes, such as boldface (by pressing **Ctrl+B**), use different justification, and so on. But usually it's faster to set attributes for an entire column with the Format Column dialog box.

Here's where you also set the justification for text within a column, as well as its appearance and size. This is often a lot faster than changing these things as you type text in cells.

### Lock Cells Whose Contents You Want Saved

If you're creating a table or form that other people will use, there may be some areas, such as the headings in columns or rows, that you don't

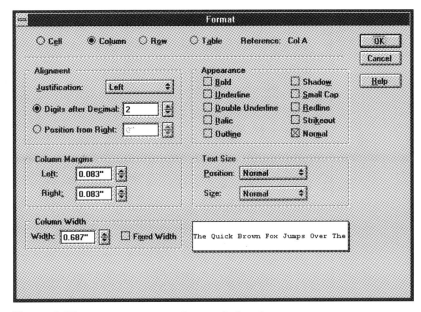

**Figure 3.47**  The Format Column dialog box

want to let folks change. You can lock those cells. Just select the cells you don't want anyone to meddle with, right-click, and choose Format and Cell. You'll see the Format Cell dialog box (Figure 3.48).

Then click Lock. From then on, nobody will be able to even put the insertion point in those cells when they're working in the regular editing screen.

### Control a Table's Position on the Page

The Table Format dialog box (Figure 3.49) lets you position the table on the page. Normally, tables are aligned on the left margin. To change this, right-click in the table, choose Format, and click the Table button. Pick a new position under Table Position.

### Tables with Different Rules or with Shaded Boxes

If you want a table to appear without rules (which WordPerfect calls "lines"), or with a rule just above and below, or with a different pattern of rules or shading in boxes, use this handy shortcut: Press **Shift+F12** when the cursor's in a table. Then pick a different pattern for your lines (Figure 3.50).

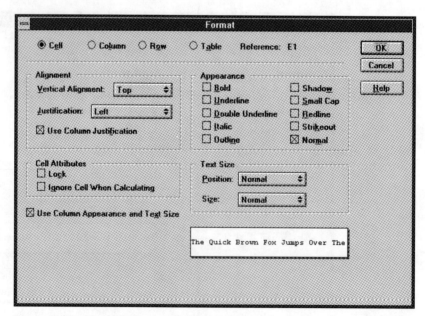

**Figure 3.48** The Format Cell dialog box

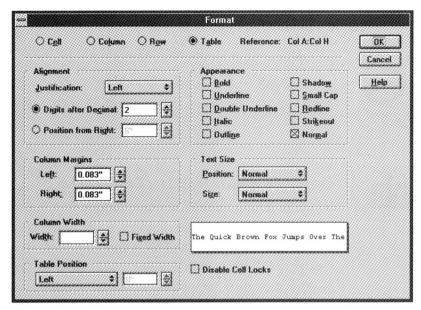

**Figure 3.49**   The Table Format dialog box

### Place Tables Side by Side

You can't put two tables side by side on a page or have text wrap around them without this tip: You must create two graphics boxes and then put the tables in them. See Chapter 7 for tips and tricks for using graphics.

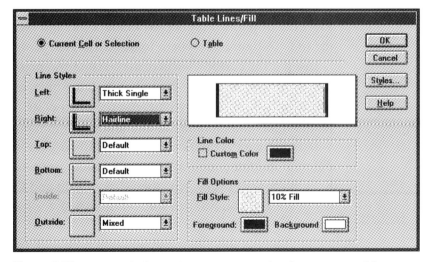

**Figure 3.50**   Press Shift+F12 to remove rules from your tables, or pick a different pattern of rules and fills.

## No More than 10% Shading in Cells with Text

If you're planning to have text in shaded cells, go light on the shading or you won't be able to read it. Heavier shading is OK in rows or columns that aren't meant to be read, but are used to separate areas of the table.

### Convert Columns to Tables for Easier Editing

If you've already typed material in columns using tabs, or if you've already set up text in parallel columns, it's easy to convert it to tables. Just select the text first and then choose Create from the Table menu. Pick either Tabular Column or Parallel Column and choose OK. You may need to do a bit of editing to the resulting table to format it as you'd like.

### Sorting Text in Tables

One of my favorite tricks. Say that you're setting up a name-and-address list, or a phone list in a table. Go ahead and input the text in any order; you can sort it alphabetically later. You can also sort it by categories like department number or zip code if you need to.

This is also a neat slick trick to use when you have to add names and addresses or phone numbers to a table later, and you don't want to take the time to figure out where to insert the new rows.

Just put the cursor anywhere in the table and press **Alt+F9**. You'll see the dialog box in Figure 3.51. If Key 1 is Alpha, as it is in this figure, you don't have to do anything else to sort the list alphabetically by the entries in the first column of the table.

If Key 1 isn't Alpha, or if you want to sort the table by entries in a different column, such as phone numbers in column 2, choose Sort **K**eys in the Sort dialog box; then choose **E**dit and **C**ell. Enter the number of the cell you want to sort on, such as **2** for Cell 2.

---

## Don't Sort a Whole Table if It Has a Heading

If there are headings in the table, you don't want to sort them! They'll wind up someplace where you don't want them. Select the cells you want to sort and *then* sort the table.

---

### Spell-Checking Checks Text in Tables

If you run the Speller on a document with tables in it, the Speller checks the text in the tables, except for text in locked cells.

If you have lots of alphanumeric entries in your tables, you might want to turn off that feature in the Speller so that the program won't query you on things like A34 and C765.

### Create Forms That Make Calculations

If you need to create, say, an invoice form that will automatically calculate totals and subtotals, figure out the tax to be added, and so forth, just set up a table in WordPerfect. You can put formulas in cells just like you can in a spreadsheet.

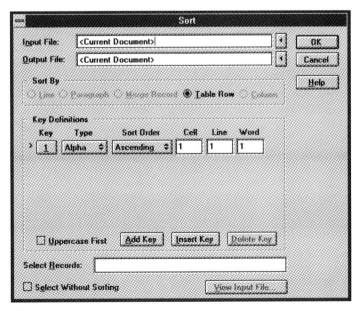

**Figure 3.51** The Sort dialog box

To enter a formula in a cell, put the cursor in the cell, right-click, and choose Formula Bar. Click in the formula bar's text box (see Figure 3.52) and type your formula (see the next tricks for more about this). Press **Enter** or click the Insert button (with the check mark) to insert the formula in the cell.

### WordPerfect's Built-In Functions Save Time

WordPerfect 6.0 comes with more than 100 built-in functions. Figure 3.53 shows a partial list. Click the Functions button on the Formula bar to see them. Although teaching about them and what they do is beyond the scope of this slick and simple tricks book, be aware that these functions are there, ready for you to use. Instead of adding up all the cells in a column individually, for example, you can use the SUM( ) function to add the contents of those cells.

For example, to sum a column:

**1** Put the cursor in the cell that's to contain the sum, say A6.

**2** Click the Functions button on the Table Formula feature bar.

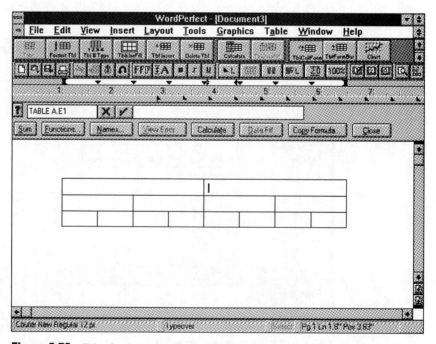

**Figure 3.52** Displaying the formula bar

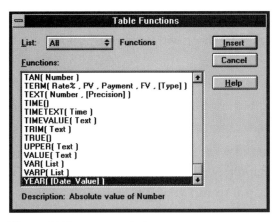

**Figure 3.53** Some of the program's built-in functions

**3** Move to the Functions list and type **s** to take you straight to the Ss. Then double-click on SUM( ).

**4** Click in the first cell in the range that you want to add up, say A2. Then drag to the end of the range you that you want to add up, say A5. Don't drag all the way to the cell that you're putting the formula in!

**5** Press **Enter** or click the Insert button.

You can also type a formula instead of choosing one. In this case, you could type **SUM(A2:A5)**. This may be faster than choosing and clicking if you can see the cells and know the exact formula ahead of time.

### *Calculating Totals, Subtotals, and Grand Totals*

Here's a shortcut for calculating subtotals, totals (the results of all subtotals), and grand totals (the results of all totals). Instead of setting up a formula that uses cell references, just enter these symbols in the Edit Formula text box, with the cursor in the cell where you want to calculate the total:

+      For a subtotal—the results of adding all the numbers in the cells directly above that cell.

=      For a total—the results of adding all the numbers in the cells with + (the subtotals) directly above.

      *    For a grand total—the results of adding all the numbers in the total cells (those with =) directly above.

# What Next?

Although we've covered a lot of formatting in this chapter, formatting is a large part of what using a word-processing program is all about. In the next chapter, we'll look at all kinds of ways you can customize WordPerfect 6.0 to suit yourself.

# Chapter 4

· · · · · · · · · · · · · · · · · · · · · · · · · ·

## Making WordPerfect 6.0
## Work Your Way

A LOT OF FOLKS WONDER WHY I urge people to try to customize a program before they're even familiar with how it works. The answer is that discovering all the neat ways you can change WordPerfect (or any other program) helps you find out just what it will and won't do. You also get a little control over the program, instead of vice versa, and that's always good for your confidence. Besides, customizing Word-Perfect is fun.

With WordPerfect 6.0, the custom-tailoring options are all over the place, instead of being located conveniently on one menu. If you used an earlier version of WordPerfect, you may remember that most customizing was done via the File menu's Setup command. Now you've got to hunt down the places where you can set your own options. Fortunately, this chapter shows you slick tricks about how you can find and use them.

# Customizing the Mouse

You can set up WordPerfect 6.0 so that your mouse feels more comfortable as you use it. If you happen to acquire a new mouse or put a modem or something on the port the mouse is normally connected to, you'll also need to tell the program about it by using the mouse setup dialog box. If your mouse is working fine, there's no need to change its settings. But just a little fine-tuning can make a big difference in your frustration level if, for example, double-clicking isn't working as you'd expect. To get to all of the mouse setup stuff quickly, exit to Windows. Click on the Mouse icon in the Windows Control Panel to get the Mouse dialog box (Figure 4.1).

Changing the tracking speed is something that you might want to do. The tracking speed controls the rate at which the mouse pointer moves on the screen as you move the mouse on your desktop. Old hands at mousing generally like a fast speed. Keep it slow until you get used to the mouse; then speed it up.

Double-clicking is another thing you'll do often in WordPerfect for Windows. If your double-clicks aren't being interpreted as double-clicks but are taken for two single clicks, change the double-click speed. Test it by double-clicking in the TEST box. How can you tell when you've got it right? The box will switch from white to black (or to white, if it's black already) when your double-clicks are being interpreted as double-clicks.

Here's also where you can make your mouse function as a (please excuse the expression) southpaw by switching the actions of the right and left mouse buttons if you're left-handed.

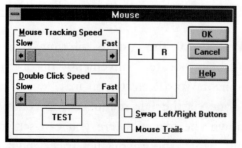

**Figure 4.1** Use the Mouse control panel to adjust the mouse

# Customizing the Screen Colors

To change screen colors in WordPerfect 6.0, you need to use the Color control panel in Windows' Program Manager (Figure 4.2). You can choose from several predefined color schemes or create your own.

When you're viewing this screen, you can just press the **Down arrow** key to see a preview of the predefined color schemes. If you like one of these, press **Enter** or click OK when it's being displayed.

You can mix your own color scheme, too. First, pick a color scheme that's close to what you want; then click on Color Palette. Then click in the Screen Element box at the top of the screen and press the **Down arrow** key to see a list of the things whose colors you can change, such as the desktop, the title bar text, the menu bar text, the scroll bars, and so forth. Then in the color palette part of the window, click on the color you want to use for that element. Then choose Save Scheme and give your color scheme a name. If you don't save it, you won't be able to use it again!

Follow a few general guidelines: Pick an easy-on-the-eyes light background color. Keep title bars and menu bars in a strong color, so you can read the words that are on them. If you want a stronger color there,

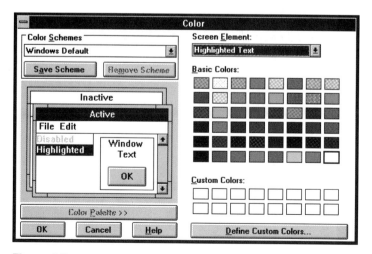

**Figure 4.2**  Use Windows' Color control panel to change the screen colors

pick one with a pattern. Remember that you need to read text on buttons and in dialog boxes, too. In scroll bars and other places where you don't have to be able to read text, you can get crazy with some of those purples and reds.

## Can't See Text in Color on the Screen?

If text on the screen isn't showing up in WordPerfect 6.0 in the color you chose in Windows, choose Preferences from the File menu and double-click the Display icon. Choose Document and make sure Windows System Colors is checked.

You can also change the color of text on the screen by pressing **Ctrl+F**, clicking Color, and picking a different color for the font to be displayed on the screen (Figure 4.3). If you change text colors this way, though, uncheck Windows System Colors.

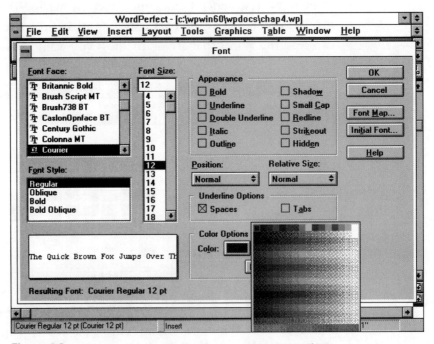

**Figure 4.3**   Use the Font dialog box to set text color

# Setting Screen Preferences

WordPerfect 6.0's display preferences (Figure 4.4) let you choose which screen elements you want to display, set the size of the Reveal Codes window, and determine whether the ruler bar appears in all your documents, among other things. Click the Display button on the Preferences button bar or choose Preferences from the File menu and double-click the Display icon to change any of these settings.

Click on any button at the top of the screen to see all the options you can set for that feature.

### Preference Button Bar Sets Preferences

There's a built-in Preferences button bar (Figure 4.5). Clicking on its buttons makes customizing your preferences fast and easy. If you're going to try a few of the tricks in this chapter, why not display it?

### Get More Screen Real Estate

If you don't like using a mouse, you probably won't use the scroll bars much either. There are keyboard tricks you can use to move through a

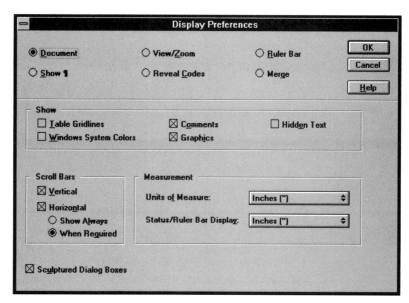

**Figure 4.4**   Setting document display preferences

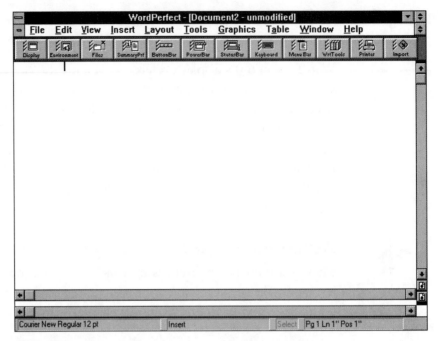

**Figure 4.5** Displaying the Preferences button bar

document—the PgUp and PgDn keys, the arrow keys, plus the Go To dialog box, to mention but a few. So if you never use the scroll bars, you may not want to display them.

### *Change Units of Measure to Suit Yourself*

If you work in desktop publishing a lot, you may be more comfortable with measurements in points ($1/72$ inch) than inches, which is WordPerfect 6.0's factory setting. On the other hand, if you're used to earlier versions of WordPerfect, you may want "WordPerfect units" (lines and columns) as the units of measure.

### *Use Different Units of Measure in Dialog Boxes and Status Line*

This is a slick trick. You can choose a different unit of measure for the status bar. That way, you can enter measurements in, say, inches in dialog boxes but have them show in points on the status line.

### WordPerfect 6.0 Converts Units of Measure

Don't ever bother taking the time to convert measurements to what the program is set for. Just enter them with an abbreviation indicating what units they're in, and WordPerfect 6.0 will convert them for you. For example, to enter 15 points and have WordPerfect 6.0 translate that to inches, if inches is the measurement that's set, enter **15p**. Here are the abbreviations to use:

| | |
|---|---|
| " or i | Inches |
| c | Centimeters |
| m | Millimeters |
| p | Points |
| w | 1/1200ths of an inch |
| u | WordPerfect 4.2 units (lines and columns) |

WordPerfect will also convert fractions to decimal equivalents. For example, if it's set for inches and you enter 3⅓, that becomes 3.33.

### Display Details in the Reveal Codes Window

Normally, a Reveal Codes window shows codes that contain other codes as abbreviated codes. For example, if you've set a header, the code normally displays as [Header A:]. To display the text that's in that header, you have to put the cursor on the code.

To have WordPerfect display the full formatting codes that are in effect all the time, click the Reveal Codes button and check the Show Codes in Detail box (Figure 4.6).

You can also pick a different color for your Reveal Codes window and specify whether or not you want it to appear automatically in all the documents you open.

## Custom-Tailoring Your Environment

In WordPerfect, the "environment" refers to an array of options, such as how the cursor moves through codes, whether warning beeps sound, what menus display, and so forth. All of these things work in the

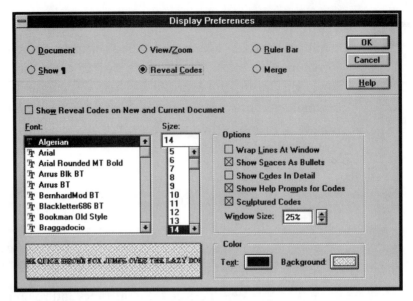

**Figure 4.6**  Setting preferences for Reveal Codes

background, so that's probably why they're called environment settings. To get to them (Figure 4.7), click the Environment button on the Preference button bar or choose Preferences from the File menu and double-click on the Environment icon.

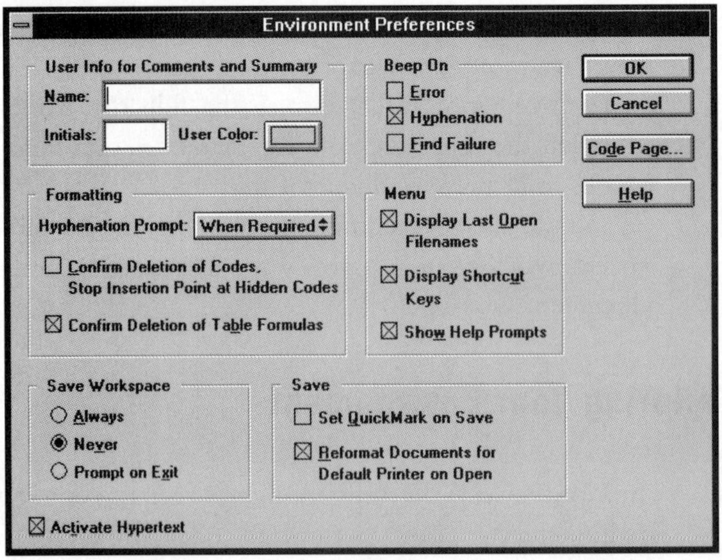

**Figure 4.7**  The environment settings you can change

### Customize the Menus

You can choose whether menus display shortcut keys and the names of the last few files you opened. If you never use shortcut keys anyway, turn 'em off for a less cluttered display. Also, once you're used to what the various things in WordPerfect 6.0 do, you might want to switch off the help prompts.

### Pick Your User Color

If you're part of a workgroup in which documents are routed for review on the screen, you can pick a color that will be used for your document comments. While you're at it, supply your initials. Don't bother with this one, though, unless you use WordPerfect's Comments feature.

### Set a QuickMark Each Time You Save

If you check that Set QuickMark on Save box, you'll always be able to find where you left off the next time you open a document.

Also, save your workspace if you want to return to the same documents you were previously working on the next time you start Word-Perfect. You saw this trick back in Chapter 1.

---

### WordPerfect Formats Documents for the Selected Printer

Why is this a Trap? Well, if you've already formatted a document for, say, a PostScript laser printer, and you happen to have a dot-matrix printer selected when you open the document, your document will be reformatted for that printer, and the PostScript fonts will be substituted with the dot-matrix fonts that are currently available.

Normally, you probably do want a document to be formatted for the printer you're using—if you're planning to print the document. But if you're retrieving it to the screen to edit or format it, you may want to keep it formatted for the printer it was intended to be used on. Uncheck the Reformat Document for Default Printer on Open box if you want the program to work this way.

# Customizing the Button Bars

A button bar lets you execute complicated tasks just by clicking on an icon. Instead of choosing from menus, pressing function keys, or remembering complicated command sequences, all you need to do is click on an icon that represents the task you want to carry out.

You can have several different button bars with icons, or buttons, that represent various tasks. For example, one could be for everyday mail-merge tasks, another could be set up for creating reference aids, such as indexes and tables of contents, and a third might have buttons that type boilerplate text and create specialized document formats. If you set up WordPerfect for other less experienced people to use, making a button bar for all the tasks they'll need to do is an excellent slick trick—they won't have to learn much about the program at all!

To customize the button bars, you can use a slick little shortcut: Right-click on the button bar and choose Preferences. Now you can pick the button bar you want to change (Figure 4.8); then click Options and set the bar up the way you want it to appear, picking a different font and size for the buttons and so forth (Figure 4.9).

It's safest to edit a copy of a button bar instead of the original. That way, it's easy to use the original, too.

### Display Button Bars to See More Buttons

If you really get into adding buttons to Button Bars, you'll soon get too many to see all of them at the top of the screen at once. When all the

**Figure 4.8**  Choosing a button bar to customize

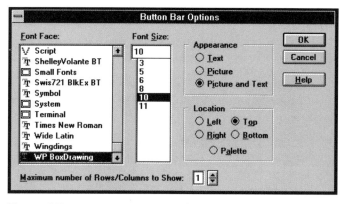

**Figure 4.9**  Button bar options

space fills up, you'll see arrows on the left side of the screen that you can use to scroll the button bar. But there's a neater way to set up the button bar.

In the Button Bar Options dialog box (Figure 4.9), you can choose different arrangements for your button bar—Picture and Text, Picture, and Text, as well as Top, Bottom, Left, Right, and Palette. If you choose Text only, you'll be able to display a lot more buttons.

### Getting the Most Buttons

To display the maximum number of buttons, choose Text and Left.

### Display a Button Bar As a Palette for Easier Editing

If you want to be able to see all the buttons on a button bar at once as you edit it, use this slick trick: Drag the button bar to the center of the screen, and it will change into a palette. Now right-click on it and choose Edit (Figure 4.10). You can easily see which spot you want to move a button to, or where you want to add a new button.

When you're done editing, drag the button bar back up to the top of the screen to put it away.

### Adding a Button to a Button Bar

To add a button to a button bar, first display the button bar you want to add to. Then right-click on it and choose Edit. Click Activate a Feature (Figure 4.11); then choose the feature you want to add. Check out

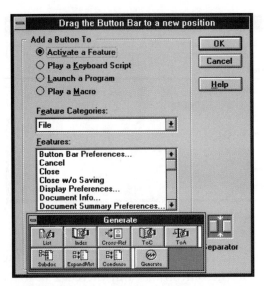

**Figure 4.10**   Editing a button bar

all the different categories to see the features you can add. To add the feature you've selected, click Add and OK.

You can edit the button bar with the mouse while the Button Bar Editor is open. Just drag a button off the button bar to delete it, or drag it to another location to reposition it.

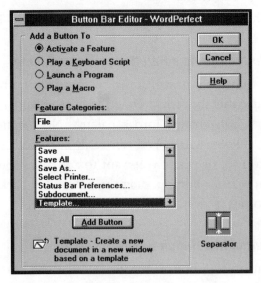

**Figure 4.11**   Adding a feature as a button

### *Have a Button Play a Keyboard Script*

If there's text you find yourself typing over and over, such as your name and address, make it into a button. Edit the button bar, choose Play a Keyboard Script, and type the text (Figure 4.12). Then click Add Script and OK to make it into a button you can click on. You may want to go back and customize the text that's on the button; by default, Word-Perfect uses the first word you typed.

---

### *Record a Macro for Long Text*

In actual practice, if there's boilerplate text you want to be able to type automatically, a better way is to create a macro that types that text, instead of assigning it to a script. You'll be able to include formatting such as boldface and italics in the text, whereas a script can't include any formatting. See the trick "Assign Macros to Buttons" later in this chapter.

---

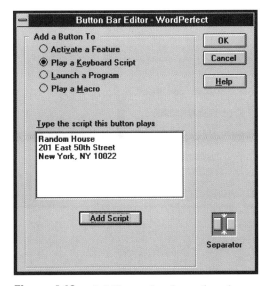

**Figure 4.12** Adding a keyboard script as a button

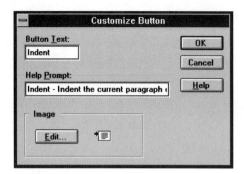

**Figure 4.13** Customizing a button's text

### *Edit the Buttons Themselves*

When the Button Bar Editor is open, double-click on any button to go to the Customize Button dialog box. You can change the help text and the prompt associated with that button, too (Figure 4.13).

To edit the button face, click Edit and you'll be taken to the image editor where you can draw a new button face or change the existing one pixel by pixel (Figure 4.14).

### *Create Your Own Custom Button Bar*

You can edit an existing Button Bar or create one from scratch. Often, it's faster to customize one that's already created than to build one from

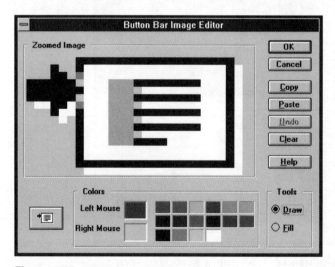

**Figure 4.14** Editing a button face

the ground up. If you want some of the same tasks on a custom button bar, copy the button bar, give the copy a different name, and then edit it. Beats building it button by button.

## Don't Put Too Many Buttons on One Button Bar

If you've customized a button bar, you may have created more buttons than the screen can display at one time. Try not to do this, or you'll defeat the purpose of being able to easily click on a button to carry out a task. Delete a few buttons you hardly use.

### Assign Macros to Buttons

You can have WordPerfect 6.0 do just about anything when you click on a button. The slick trick here is to assign a macro to the button. For example, say that you've recorded a macro that formats and types your letterhead, and you'd like to be able to create your letterhead at the click of a button. You can add WordPerfect's built-in macros to button bars, too. Here's how to add the Dropcap macro to your button bar.

1. Display the button bar you want to add the macro to.

2. Click on it with the right mouse button and choose Edit.

3. Choose Play a Macro in the Add a Button list; then click Add Macro.

4. Press **Alt+Down arrow** to see a list of the prerecorded macros.

5. Double-click on the macro's name (in this case, dropcap.wcm) and click Select. Say Yes to the prompt about saving with the full path.

You'll see the new generic macro icon on your button bar. Double-click on it to give it some descriptive text, as you saw in an earlier trick. You can edit its face, too.

### Set Up Button Bars for Specialized Tasks

A lot of folks think that buttons should be for things they do a lot of the time. But the reverse is also true: Buttons are very handy for things you hardly ever do and don't want to remember how to do them! Remember, if you turn on the macro recorder, WordPerfect faithfully records everything you do, and you can make that macro into a button! So, for the next complicated procedure—defining an index style, for example—record the process as a macro and assign it to a button. That way, you'll never have to figure out how to do it again.

### *Assign a Button Bar to a Document*

If there's a specialized button bar you use with only one document, such as a weekly report you create over and over, you can have Word-Perfect open that button bar with only that document each time you work on it. To do this, you'll need to make that document into a template.

Choose **Template** from the **File** menu or press **Ctrl+T** (Figure 4.15). Choose Options and Create Template (Figure 4.16). Give your template a name; then click OK. To create the button bar, click Create Object and Button Bar. Add the buttons you want that button bar to have, as you've seen in previous tricks. Click Exit Template and save your template.

Now, when you want to create one of those weekly reports, press **Ctrl+T** and choose that template. It will open with the custom button bar you set up.

**Figure 4.15**  Choosing a template

**Figure 4.16**   Creating a new template

### *Use a Button to Go to Button Bars*

It's easy to switch from one Button Bar to another if you use this slick trick: Put a button on the Button Bar that will take you to another Button Bar when you click on it. Just record a macro that switches you to that button bar and assign it to a button!

### *A Button Takes You Back to the Main Button Bar*

Don't make buttons a one-way street! If you're customizing Button Bars and adding buttons that access other Button Bars, why not add a button that quickly takes you back to the main Button Bar when you're through using your specialized button bar? Make that button one that opens the WordPerfect Button Bar.

### *Button Ideas*

What kinds of things might you want to make buttons for? Here are some easy choices:

- ♦ The Reveal Codes window
- ♦ The Select Printer command (if you have more than one printer)
- ♦ Next Window (if you have trouble remembering **Ctrl+F6**)
- ♦ Switching to a particular font and point size if you do that frequently (use a macro for this)

Remember, if there are buttons you never use on the preset Button Bars, remove them to make room for your own.

### *A Button or Menu Item Can Launch Another Program*

If there's another program you use frequently from within WordPerfect 6.0, why not make a button that launches it, as you've seen in an earlier trick, or put a command on the menu for it, as you'll see in the next tricks? As you're editing a button bar, power bar, or menu bar, just choose Launch a Program from the Activate a Feature list; then choose Select File and pick the program you want to be able to launch from within WordPerfect 6.0. Programs have a .COM or .EXE extension. You can choose a batch file, too (one with a .BAT extension).

# Customizing the Other Bars

WordPerfect 6.0 will let you customize other bars, too—the power bar, the status bar, the menu bar, and so forth. You can assign a feature, a script, or a macro to a button, or make a button that launches a program or executes a batch file. Or you can put any of these kinds of commands directly on the menu bar.

### Customizing the Power Bar

It's easy to customize the power bar, too. You can choose which buttons will show up on it and change the way it looks. Click the Power Bar button on the Preferences button bar to get to the Power Bar Preferences dialog box (Figure 4.17).

If there are features you never use on the power bar, drag 'em off while the Power Bar Preferences dialog box is open. Rearrange the

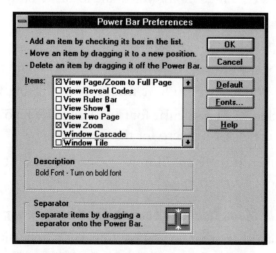

**Figure 4.17**   Customizing the power bar

buttons so that the ones you use most often are within easy reach. Add buttons for what you *do* use if they're not there already.

### Customizing the Status Bar

Want your status bar to display the date and time (Figure 4.18) or indicate whether Caps Lock or Num Lock is on? Click the Status Bar button on the Preferences button bar and choose what you want on your status bar (Figure 4.19).

You may need to remove an item or two to make room for your new choices.

### Customizing the Menus

Click the Menu Bar button on the Preferences button bar to customize WordPerfect's menu system. But for safety's sake, edit a copy of the standard menu system (you can't edit a predefined menu bar anyway). Choose <WPWin 6.0 Menu> and click Copy. Leave the templates to copy To and From set to standard; then highlight <WPWin 6.0 Menu> in the Select Menu Bars to Copy box and click Copy again. In the

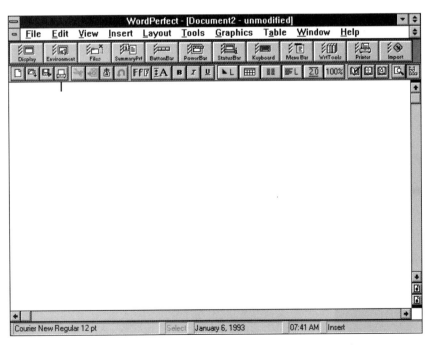

**Figure 4.18** **Displaying the date and time on the status bar**

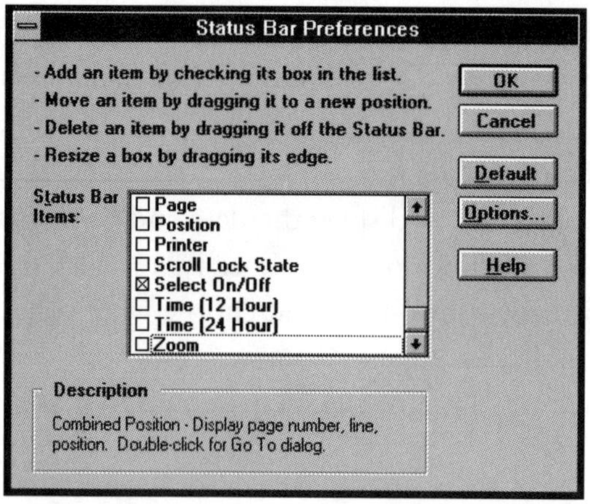

**Figure 4.19**   The Status Bar Preferences
dialog box

Overwrite/New Name dialog box, give your new menu system a new name. Now highlight that name and click Edit to customize it.

Now you can go crazy. Choose Activate a Feature; then drag whatever feature you want to the menu bar and drop it. That puts the item on the main menu.

If you want to move a command from one menu to another, just drag it over there. To delete a command from the menu bar, drag it off the screen.

To create your own cascading menu, drag the Menu icon in the lower right corner of the dialog box to the menu bar. Then add items to it by dragging them. Drag the Separator icon to add dividing lines to your new cascading menu. You can really spend some time with this and get the menus just the way you want them.

### *Change Text on Menus, Too*

To customize the text that's displayed on menus, double-click on the item you want to change in the Menu Bar Editor. Actually open the menu and double-click on the command; don't click in the dialog box! Then, in the Edit Menu Text dialog box (Figure 4.20), change the text to what you want it to read. If you want a shortcut for the command to be available, type an ampersand (&) just before the letter you want to use as the shortcut.

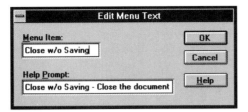

**Figure 4.20**   Changing the text of a command

### *Resetting a Menu to the Way It Was*

Use this slick trick to set a menu back to its factory settings: Press **Ctrl+Alt+Shift+Backspace**. If WordPerfect won't start after you've customized a bunch of things (this happened to me), use the command **wpwin /x** to start it.

# Customizing Your Keyboard

WordPerfect 6.0 comes with three different keyboard layouts:

♦ The WPWin 6.0 keyboard is the one that corresponds to the function-key template you received with the program.

♦ The Equation Editor keyboard lets you easily type Greek letters and commonly used symbols. **Ctrl+A**, for example, produces a lowercase Greek alpha ($\alpha$) and **Ctrl+B** produces a lowercase Greek beta ($\beta$).

♦ The WPDOS Compatible keyboard uses the same keystrokes that are used in the DOS version of WordPerfect. **Home Home Up arrow** takes you to the beginning of the document, for example.

To switch from one keyboard to another (Figure 4.21), click the Keyboard button on the Preferences button bar or choose Preferences from the File menu and double-click on the Keyboard icon.

Now, don't think that your keyboard is going to physically change when you switch keyboards. All that happens is that pressing key combinations produces different results, depending on which keyboard is in effect.

You can also create custom keyboards, which is a pretty sophisticated thing to do, but I'll show you a few easy slick tricks you can use for that, too.

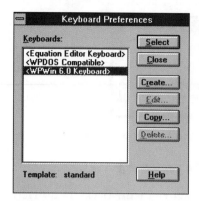

**Figure 4.21** WordPerfect's
built-in keyboards

### Create the Custom Keyboard You Want

WordPerfect won't let you edit one of the original keyboards; you have
to create a new one by basing it on an original keyboard. Choose the
keyboard that's closest to the new custom keyboard you want to create;
then click Create. Give your new keyboard a new name. You'll wind up
in the Keyboard Editor (Figure 4.22), where you can assign a program,
a command, a script, or a macro to keys, and move key assignments
around and create keyboard shortcuts to your heart's content.

### Assign a Special Symbol to a Key

If there are special symbols you use regularly, assign them to a key combination. Choose Allow Assignments to Characters; then select the key
or key combination you want to use. Select Play a Keyboard Script,
press **Ctrl+W**, and choose the symbol you want from one of WordPerfect's character sets. Now choose Assign.

### Resetting a Keyboard to the Way It Was

It's easy to mess up a keyboard definition. It's even easier to forget
which keys you assigned to what. If you get confused, you can always
go back to the default keyboard. To reset a keyboard definition back
to the default, press **Ctrl+Alt+Shift+Backspace** while you're in a
document.

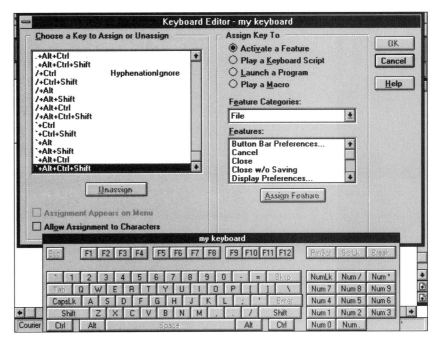

**Figure 4.22** The Keyboard Editor

# Now What?

· · · · · · · · · · · · · · · · · · · · · · · · · · · · · · · · · · · · ·

We've covered all kinds of slick tricks for customizing WordPerfect 6.0, but not all of them—not by a long shot. For example, you can set preferences about which directories to use for what, how QuickLists work, what system of filenames and extensions you prefer, and more. You'll find tricks for these in the next chapter, which is all about file management.

# Chapter 5

· · · · · · · · · · · · · · · · · · · · · · · · · · · ·

## Tricks for Managing Files

YOU DON'T JUST CREATE AND EDIT DOCUMENTS in WordPerfect; you also have to keep track of them. WordPerfect 6.0 has done away with the File Manager you may have seen in earlier versions and now lets you create new directories and rename, copy, and delete files, or move them from one directory to another right in any file management dialog box, such as an Open, Save as, or Insert File dialog box. In addition, it has very sophisticated search features that let you locate files by name or by what's in them.

### *Where the Files Are*

If you're not sure about where files are stored on your hard disk, try this trick. Click the Files button in the Preferences button bar; then click View All. You'll see which directories WordPerfect is storing your files in (Figure 5.1).

145

## The ABCs of Your Directory System

On your hard disk, you put files into a system of *directories,* just as you stuff paper files in manila file folders in a filing cabinet in your office. A directory can hold all different kinds of files, such as word-processing programs (e.g., WordPerfect), spreadsheet programs (e.g., Lotus 1-2-3 or Microsoft Excel), documents you create, spreadsheets, and graphics. A directory can also contain other directories, called *subdirectories,* just as though you stuffed one file folder inside another.

If you stuff a lot of folders inside folders (in other words, have a lot of subdirectories under a directory), you can easily get lost when you want to find what you're looking for in a particular subdirectory. Your computer can get lost, too, so it lets you use a command called PATH (in your AUTOEXEC.BAT file) that tells your system where to look for programs. When you installed WordPerfect, it most likely set up your path to tell your computer where your WordPerfect program is, so you don't have to worry about that. What you *do* need to know about your path is the rather cryptic way you have to write it out: Each subdirectory is separated from the next higher-level subdirectory by a backslash, and your hard disk drive's letter is followed by a colon. So, this is what the path to your WordPerfect directory probably looks like, assuming that drive C is your hard drive:

C:\WPWIN60

If you haven't changed anything since you installed WordPerfect, your documents are probably stored in a directory named WPDOCS under your WPWIN60 directory. Its path would look like this:

C:\WPWIN60\WPDOCS

You'll need to use this type of path notation if you want to save documents in different directories, or change directories to open or retrieve a file that's in a different directory, so it's good to have a little basic understanding of how it works.

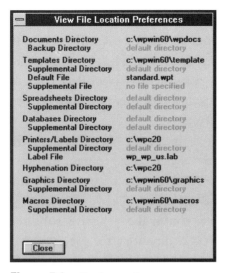

**Figure 5.1** Seeing where your files are stored

### *Change the Program's Preset Directories*

To change the directory that the program will automatically send your documents to, click the Files button on the Preferences button bar. Next to Documents/Backup Default Directory (Figure 5.2), type a new path name. For example, you might rather store your documents in

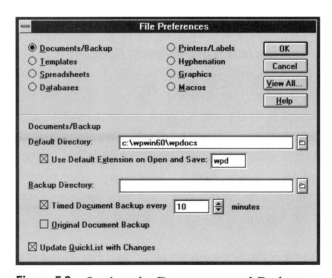

**Figure 5.2** Setting the Documents and Backup directories

directory C:\WP51\DOCS because that's where your older Word-Perfect 5.1 documents are stored. WordPerfect 6.0 will automatically open WordPerfect 5.1 documents, but be warned that if you save them as WordPerfect 6.0 documents—WordPerfect 5.1 can't open them. You'll have to go back and save them as WordPerfect 5.1 documents by using the Save As command.

Most of the time, you'll leave WordPerfect's files alone and keep them in the directories where the program expects to find them. But the C:\WPWIN60\WPDOCS directory can get quite full in a hurry if you put into it all the document files you create.

My advice is that you make separate subdirectories under that C:\WPWIN60\WPDOCS directory for specialized documents, such as letters, reports, and invoices. Or keep client files in separate subdirectories. Or organize your files by project. Pick a scheme that lets you keep track of where your files are. Believe me, if you put everything in C:\WPWIN60\WPDOCS, it will get huge in a hurry. You'll get tired of looking in that huge directory all the time, and you'll find it hard to find things quickly (see the next trick).

Having documents in separate directories also makes backups easier. I keep files in subdirectories by project. Normally, I work on only one project a day, so I can easily make a backup of my daily work on a floppy disk just by copying the files in the current directory that have today's date.

### Storing a Document in a Different Directory

You don't *have* to change the default directory to be able to store documents in a different directory. All you have to do, the first time you save a document, is specify the path to the directory where you want to save it. For example, if I want to store a file in my C:\WP51\DOCS directory, I just type c:\wp51\docs\*filename* when I'm prompted for a document name. Once you've saved a document under a certain name, WordPerfect remembers where you want to store it so that you don't have to type all that out again each time you save it.

### Create Directories without Windows File Manager or DOS

You don't have to go out to the Windows File Manager or to DOS to create a new directory in WordPerfect. Click the File Options button in any file management dialog box, and you'll see a list of all kinds of things that you can do right there (Figure 5.3).

### A Fast Trip to DOS

WordPerfect comes with a Gotodos macro. Run it to open a DOS window if you have to go to DOS. It's faster than going to the Program Manager and then going to the DOS prompt. Press **Alt+F10**, enter gotodos, and press **Enter**.

### Changing Directories

To switch to looking at what's in a different directory once you're viewing a file management dialog box, just double-click on the directory's name. You can also highlight it and press **Enter**.

If you can't see the directory you want to change to, click on a folder higher up in the chain under Directories. You may need to go all the way back to the root directory, c:\, and then go down the chain again to find the directory you want to look into. Click on the arrow under Drives to see what's on a different drive, such as your floppy drive a:.

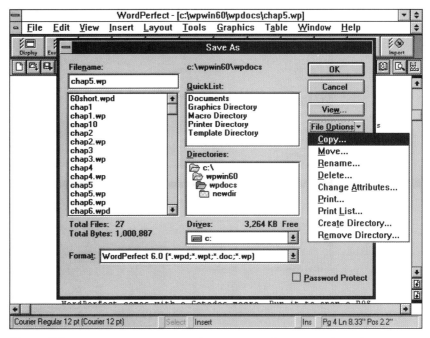

**Figure 5.3** File management jobs you can do in WordPerfect

### Quick Moves in a File List

Use the **PgDn** and **PgUp** keys, **Home**, and **End** to move quickly through a long list of files in a file management dialog box.

To go quickly to part of the alphabet, type the letter you want to go to. This slick trick is handy for quickly getting down to the Ws.

### Look in Files without Opening Them

When a filename is highlighted in a file management dialog box, just click the View button. You'll see a Viewer window (Figure 5.4). Click on a filename to see what's in it. You can view graphics files this way, too, which is really convenient for reviewing what's in your graphics files.

### Viewer Window Shows More Options

If you click with the right mouse button on a Viewer window, you'll see more options you can choose (Figure 5.5).

Select Viewer Setup to have WordPerfect 6.0 automatically convert graphics files to a format it can display in a Viewer window.

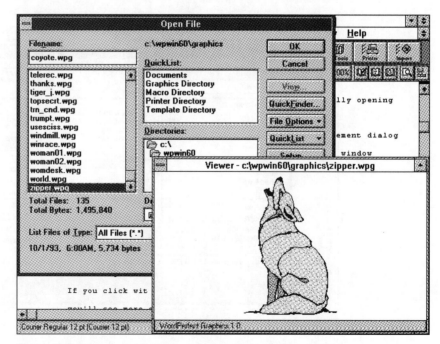

**Figure 5.4** You can see what's in a file without opening it.

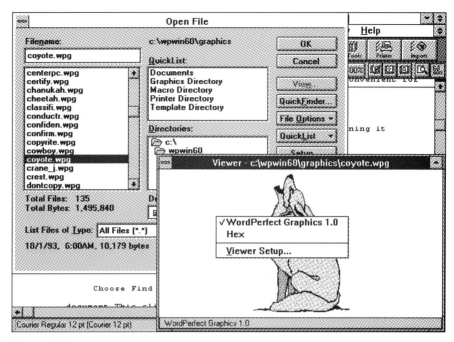

**Figure 5.5** More options in a Viewer window

### *Search the Text within a File*

When you're viewing the contents of a text file, you'll see different options when you right-click in a Viewer window (Figure 5.6). Choose Find or press **F2** to search for text within that document. This slick trick can really refine your searches, because you can make sure that the document you're viewing is exactly the one you want before retrieving it to the editing screen.

### *Copy Text from a Viewer Window*

If you want to copy some text from a document into a different document, but you don't know which document the text is in, use the Viewer window to see into various documents until you find the one you want. Then copy the text with **Ctrl+C** and paste it where you want it in your document. It's faster than opening up a bunch of different documents!

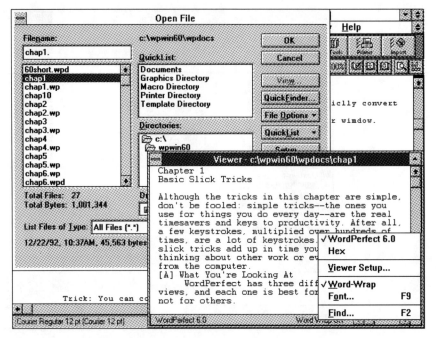

**Figure 5.6** Options for viewing text files

### Right-Click in Various Lists

You can right-click in a file list, directories, or QuickList, which brings up a QuickMenu of more options you can choose (See Figures 5.7 through 5.9). It's usually faster than clicking an Options button.

### Force Frequently Used Filenames to the Tops of Lists

Since WordPerfect normally lists files alphanumerically, with numbers first, just name any file you use frequently to begin with a number instead of a letter. For example, if you're working on a book, name the chapters 1CH and 2CH instead of CH1 and CH2 so that they won't slide down into the Cs.

If you use descriptive names (see the trick "Descriptive Names Help Find Documents More Efficiently" later in the chapter), you can use this trick, too. With descriptive names, you can use spaces so that documents can have names like 1 Basic Tricks Chapter and 2 Editing Tricks Chapter.

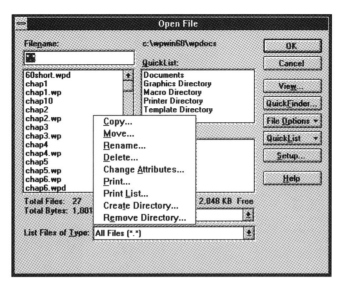

**Figure 5.7**  The file list QuickMenu

### *Change the Way You Look at Files*

Normally, WordPerfect lists files alphabetically, with directories at the top of the list. Sometimes it's nicer to see the files you worked with most recently listed first, though. And sometimes you may not want to look at *all* the files, especially in a big directory, except those ending in .WPG (graphics files) or some other special extension.

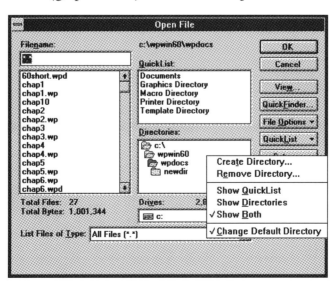

**Figure 5.8**  The directories list QuickMenu

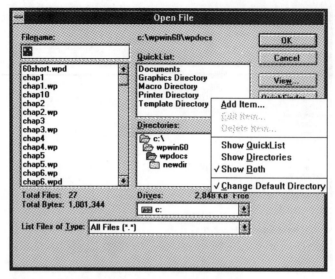

**Figure 5.9** The QuickList QuickMenu

You can click the Setup button (or right-click in a file list and choose Setup) in a file management dialog box, and then choose Sort By to tell WordPerfect to sort your list by date, by extension, and so forth (Figure 5.10).

Click Show to choose whether you want to see just filenames, or the size, date, and time of creation, or even set up custom columns and use descriptive names (see the tricks "Using Speedup Files" and "Descriptive Names Help Find Documents More Efficiently" later in the chapter).

### Using Custom Columns

Using custom columns lets you tailor file management dialog boxes exactly the way you like them. You can rearrange the order of columns so

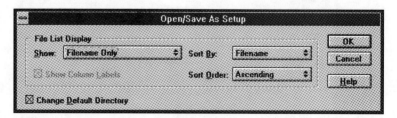

**Figure 5.10** Setting setup options for a file management dialog box

that the date comes first, for example. If you decide to set up custom columns in your file management dialog boxes, here are some tricks for using them:

♦ To delete a column, just drag its column label away.

♦ To move a column to a different position, drag its column label.

♦ To change a column's width, drag the edge of the column label.

### Using Speedup Files

If you choose custom columns or descriptive names as a Show option, the dialog box you're looking at will give you speedup options (Figure 5.11). If you choose to create speedup files, WordPerfect stores all the descriptive information about your file as a separate file, instead of storing it in the document summary part of the file. This will speed up displaying file lists and information about your files. If you don't use document summaries or descriptive names, there's no point in turning this feature on, though.

### Descriptive Names Help Find Documents More Efficiently

DOS requires that you use only eight characters plus a three-character extension for filenames, which really doesn't help a lot if you're looking at a list of files named LTTR1.WPD and LTTR2.WPD, or even FEBLETTR.WPD. You can use longer descriptive names that actually describe what's in your documents, such as the ones in Figure 5.12.

To use descriptive names, you'll have to use document summaries. Choose Document Summary from the File menu. In the Document

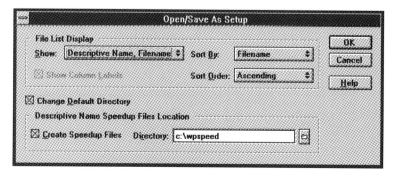

**Figure 5.11**   Choosing Speedup options

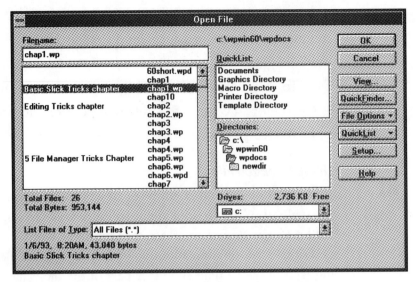

**Figure 5.12**   Using descriptive names

Summary dialog box, give your document a descriptive name (Figure 5.13). Any documents that you *don't* give descriptive names will continue to be displayed as their regular DOS filenames in file management dialog boxes.

Now go back to the trick "Change the Way You Look at Files" to see how to set up a file management dialog box to show descriptive filenames.

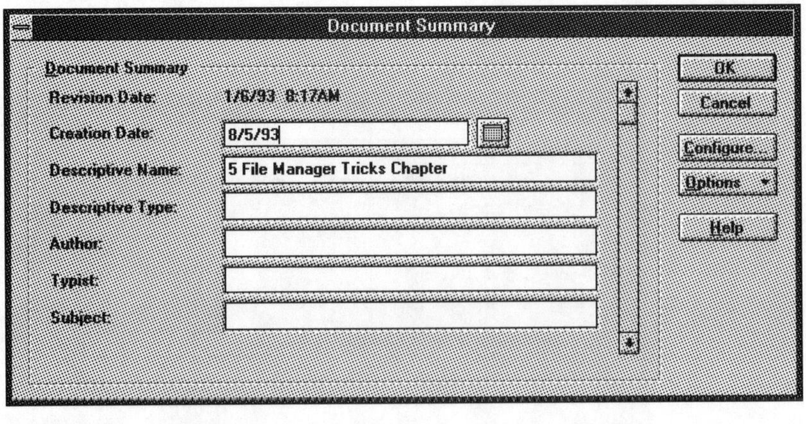

**Figure 5.13**   Assigning a descriptive name to a document

### WordPerfect 6.0 Can Automatically Display Descriptive Names

You'll need to take one final step to tell the program to display descriptive names automatically when you save or open documents. Click the SummaryPref button on the Preferences button bar. In the dialog box that you'll see (Figure 5.14), check Use Descriptive Names.

Also, check the Create Summary on Save/Exit if you want to be prompted to enter a descriptive name for a document the first time you save it.

For more document summary tricks, see the section on document summaries toward the end of this chapter.

### Print from a File Management Dialog Box

Instead of going back to the editing screen to print a document, you can print it from a file management dialog box. In fact, you can select several files at once and send them all to the printer, which is much faster than displaying each document on the screen and sending it to the printer individually.

### Need Disk Labels? Print File Lists.

It's often useful to print out the contents of a floppy disk and then use the printout as a label on the disk itself. You can print entire file lists, or you can select certain files and just print a list of them.

Display the file management dialog box's options by right-clicking on a file list; then Choose Print List to print out a copy of the directory list you're displaying or the filenames you've selected.

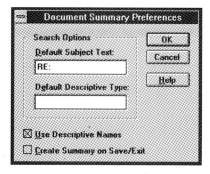

**Figure 5.14**   Making WordPerfect display descriptive names on opening or saving

### Alt+Down Arrow Opens a File List

Some dialog boxes have file lists built into them. In these, you'll see a tiny folder icon. To open one of these file lists quickly, click on that icon or put the cursor in the text box and press **Alt+Down arrow**.

### Different Ways to the Open Dialog Box

Opening documents is one thing you'll do a *lot* of in WordPerfect, so there are several different routes to the Open dialog box:

- Press **Ctrl+O**
- Press **F4**
- Choose **O**pen from the **F**ile menu
- Click the Open Document button on the power bar

### Listing Possible Files to Open

The easiest thing to do if you know the first letter of a document's name is to move to the file list part of the Open dialog box and type that letter to go straight to that part of the alphabet. This is handy in long lists where the document you want may not be displayed on the screen.

### Avoid Hunting for Files by Typing a Path Name

If you know where the file you want is, you can save a lot of time by typing its path name in a Filename text box, instead of hunting for it in your directory system. For example, if you know that the document you want is stored in your C:\WP51\DOCS directory and its name is MAYLTTR, enter C:\WP51\DOCS\MAYLTTR. To see all the files beginning with M in that directory, use C:\WP51\DOCS\M*.* (See the sidebar "Using Wildcards" later in the chapter.)

### Selecting Several Files at Once

You can select several files at the same time in a file list. Just drag over files that are next to each other to select them. Or **Shift-click**: Press **Shift** and click on the first one; then keep **Shift** down and click on the last one. **Ctrl-click** to select files that aren't next to each other. Now you can copy them, delete them, open them, or whatever you want to do, all at once. Saves you a lot of time.

### Ctrl+/ Selects All Files in a Directory

Press **Ctrl+/** to select all the files in a directory. If you're selecting *most* of the files, select all of them and then deselect the few you don't want by **Ctrl-clicking** on those.

### QuickLists Locate Files Used Frequently

The QuickList (Figure 5.15) is a neat feature that lets you specify which files and directories you work with most often so that you don't have to go hunting through your whole directory system.

To set up your own QuickList, go to any file management dialog box (use the Open, Save As, or Insert File commands); then click the Quick-List button to get a drop-down menu. Choose Show QuickList, Show Directories, or Both (both are shown in Figure 5.15).

The first time you use the QuickList feature, you'll see placeholders for the basic types of files. You may not need all of these categories; you can delete the ones you'll probably never use, as you'll see in a later trick.

To add a new item to your QuickList, right-click on it and choose Add Item. You'll see the Add QuickLIst Item dialog box (Figure 5.16). Click on the directory icon to see your filing system. Just double-click

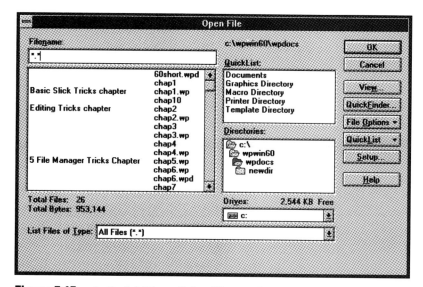

**Figure 5.15**   **A QuickList of the files and directories the author works with frequently**

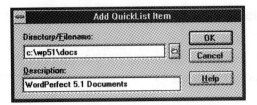

**Figure 5.16** Adding an item to the QuickList

on the name of the directory or file you want added to the QuickList, or type its path.

Enter a descriptive name for the item, too. You can use upper- and lowercase as well as spaces in QuickList names. Be descriptive so that you can find things easily.

You can add directories, individual documents, or lists of certain kinds of files to a QuickList (see the next tricks).

### Put Documents in Your QuickList

You'd think from looking at the QuickList dialog box that comes with WordPerfect that the best thing to do with a QuickList is add directories to it. I find that it's a lot handier to add documents, not directories, to a QuickList.

### Add All Kinds of Documents to a QuickList

The directory you add doesn't have to be a WordPerfect directory! If you work with documents stored in a C:\WINWORD or C:\LOTUS \BUDGETS directory, put them on there, too, so those documents will be easy to retrieve into WordPerfect.

### Add Documents to a QuickList All at Once

You can use wildcards (see the sidebar "Using Wildcards" later in the chapter) to put patterns of document names in your QuickList.

Say that you'd like to create a QuickList item of all the personal letters that are stored in your document directory. The trick to this trick is to use special extensions to name those files. For example, you might want to use .ltr for letters, .rpt for reports, or an abbreviation of a project's name for documents related to that project. If you do this, you can quickly put those documents in your QuickList by category. (If you haven't set up a system of extensions before, you can go back and re-name those files by using the Rename option in a file management dialog box.)

For example, to set up a category for letters that have the extension .ltr in your C:\WPWIN60\WPDOCS directory, you'd type **Personal Letters** in the Description box and **C:\WPWIN60\WPDOCS\\*.LTR** in the Directory/Filename box.

### QuickList Tricks

Once you've set up a QuickList, use these tricks:

♦ Double-click on a directory in a QuickList to see the files in that directory.

♦ Double-click on a filename in a QuickList to open that document.

♦ Click with the right mouse button in the QuickList to edit or delete an item.

## Copying, Renaming, and Deleting Files

One neat thing about WordPerfect's new file management system is that it lets you do a lot of file housekeeping that you'd normally have to use the Windows File Manager for. In a file management dialog box,

---

**Using Wildcards**

Just as in poker, *wildcards* are special characters that can stand for other characters like wild cards stand for other cards. The asterisk (*) represents any number of letters (or none at all), and the question mark (?) represents any one character (or none at all). So, *.* stands for "everything" (any or all of the eight characters in a filename plus any three-character extension) and ?LTTR.DOC stands for any files that begin with one character and are followed by LTTR.DOC, such as 1LTTR.DOC, ALTTR.DOC, and so forth. You can use wildcards to speed up operations on files that have similar name patterns so that you can manipulate several files at a time.

you can copy, move, rename, and even delete whole groups of files at once. The next slick tricks will show you how.

### Deselecting Files

To unmark files you've selected, press **Ctrl** and click on them.

### Copying and Renaming a File at the Same Time

Suppose you start out with a document named CHAP1.WPD in your C:\WPWIN60\WPDOCS directory. If you want to make a duplicate of a document in the same directory, press **Ctrl+O** to open the Open dialog box. Then select it, right-click on the list or click File Options, choose **C**opy, and give it a different filename (Figure 5.17). To make a duplicate of it in a different directory, type a new directory name and keep its filename the same (Figure 5.18). To make a duplicate of it in a different directory *and* under a different name, change both the directory name and the filename (Figure 5.19).

### Using Wildcards to Copy Files

If you want to copy all the files in a directory that have similar patterns to their names, such as all the files ending in .LTR or beginning with CH (CH1, CH2, and so on), use wildcards instead of marking each file. After you choose Copy, enter a wildcard pattern in the Copy File dialog box. For example, entering *.ltr copies all the documents with a .ltr extension, and entering ch?? copies all the files starting with CH and ending with 1, 2, 10, 11, on up to 99.

### Moving Files

If you want to move a file or files from one directory to another, mark them first and then right-click and choose **M**ove. You'll get a dialog box

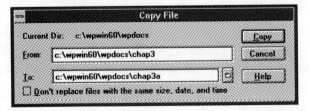

**Figure 5.17**   **Copying a file in the same directory**

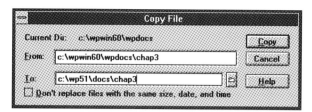

**Figure 5.18**   Copying a file into a different directory

similar to the one in Figure 5.20. Fill it out with the path name of the directory where you want to move the files.

### Create a New Directory When You Copy or Move Files

WordPerfect for Windows lets you create a new directory when you copy or move files (but WordPerfect 6.0 for DOS doesn't). Just enter the name of the directory you want to create as part of the file's path name, and you'll be asked whether you want WordPerfect to create that directory for you.

### Renaming a File and Moving It, Too

You can rename files from a file management dialog box, too. To rename a file, select it, click the right mouse button, and choose Rename. To rename the file and move it at the same time, give it a new name and specify a different directory.

### Deleting Files Quickly

You can delete whole bunches of files all at once in a file management dialog box. Select them and then press the **Del** key and **Enter**. Don't bother with menus and mouse clicks.

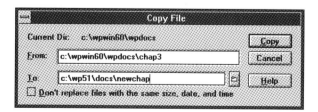

**Figure 5.19**   Copying a file into a different directory and renaming it at the same time

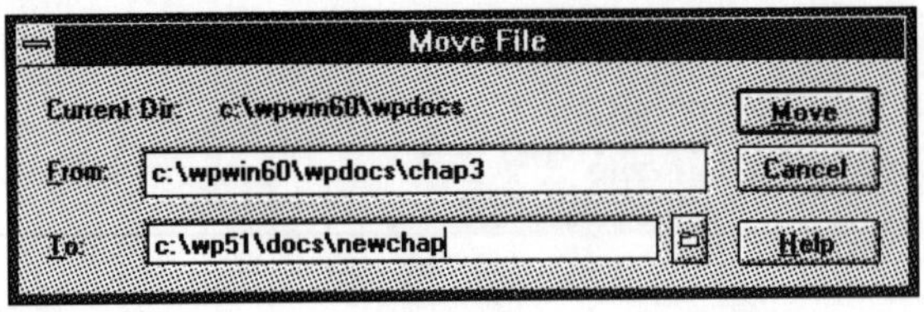

| Move File | | |
| --- | --- | --- |
| Current Dir:   c:\wpwin60\wpdocs | | **Move** |
| From:  c:\wpwin60\wpdocs\chap3 | | **Cancel** |
| To:  c:\wp51\docs\newchap | | **Help** |

**Figure 5.20**   Moving files

### Rename Files One at a Time

 You can rename files from a file management dialog box, as long as you rename them one at a time. If you've marked several files, Word-Perfect assumes you want to move them to a different directory and further assumes that the new directory is the first name you typed in the To box. It will create that directory for you (prompting you first) and then move the files that you marked to that directory.

### Be Careful When Deleting Directories

WordPerfect lets you delete directories, but be sure that's what you want to do, because it will let you delete directories *with files in them*. You'll get a warning prompt, but if you say Yes, it will go ahead and delete the directory and its files. Highlight a directory and press **Del** to delete it. You'll be asked to confirm.

# QuickFinder Tricks

WordPerfect's file management dialog boxes have a built-in QuickFin-der button that lets you locate documents by filename as well as by what's in the text inside them. But don't mix up QuickList with the QuickFinder! The QuickFinder is a special tool that builds indexes of the words in your documents. Once it's built an index on the docu-ments you specify, you can use it to locate any word or phrase in those documents really quickly. Using the QuickFinder is much faster than searching through the documents themselves. If you need to search documents frequently, use the QuickFinder to speed up your searches. This feature is great for those times when you know you wrote a letter to Aunt Martha but you can't remember the name you gave the document.

### *Simple Searching with QuickFinder*

Most of the time, you'll probably use QuickFinder to locate files by name rather than by their contents. To do this, enter a filename pattern in the File Pattern box (Figure 5.21). Enter *something* in that File Pattern box. The pattern that's there (*.*) means "everything," and you don't want to search for everything!

For example, if you know the file ends in .TEM, enter *.TEM. Or, to see all the files starting with MAR, enter MAR*.*. You can even search for several patterns at once by separating them with a space. For example, entering *.TEM A*.* *.DOC searches for all files ending in .TEM, beginning with A, or ending in .DOC.

In the Search In box, choose where you want WordPerfect to search—the current directory, the current directory plus its subdirectories (the subtree), the disk you specify, and so forth.

To restrict the files that QuickFinder locates to ones that were created or edited after a certain date, put a date in the From box under Date Range. Leave the To box blank if you want to search all the way through today's date.

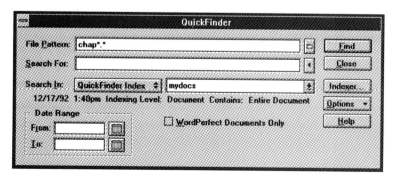

**Figure 5.21** The QuickFinder dialog box lets you search files by name and by contents.

To search just for WordPerfect documents that meet your specifications, click that tiny WordPerfect Documents Only box. This can greatly speed up your searches on a big hard disk.

### Sophisticated Searching with QuickFinder

You can have QuickFinder do some very sophisticated searching through your files. To do this, enter the words you're searching for in the Search For text box, using the special operators in Table 5.1. You can also press **F4** when the cursor's in the Search For box to display even more options to use.

### Search for an Exact Phrase with Quotation Marks

If you want the program to locate an exact phrase, put quotation marks around it, as in "this very phrase." Otherwise, the program will locate any documents that contain the words *this, very,* and *phrase,* in any order, even separated from one another.

### Search for Special Characters, Too

If you know that the document you're looking for has a special character in it, such as ¶, search for that character. It's highly likely that this

### Table 5.1   Entering Search Patterns in QuickFinder

| Enter | To Find Documents Containing |
| --- | --- |
| file | The word *file* |
| file & folder | The word *file* and the word *folder* |
| file AND folder | The word *file* and the word *folder* |
| file OR folder | The word *file* or the word *folder* |
| file I folder | The word *file* or the word *folder* |
| "file folder" | The phrase *file folder* |
| file! folder | Locates documents that contain the word *file* but not the word *folder* |
| file..folder | Locates documents that contain both the word *file* and the word *folder,* with *file* occurring first |
| n*n | The words *non, Nan, noon, northwestern,* etc. (* matches any letters) |
| n?n | The words *non, Nan, nun,* etc. (? matches any one letter) |

tip can really refine your searches, as you probably don't use special characters in very many of the documents you create. The trick is to press **Ctrl+W** and then choose the character from one of WordPerfect's character sets while the cursor is in the Search For text box.

### Two Ways to Think About Finding Files

If you're searching the contents of a file in the QuickFinder's Search For box, enter *as much text as you can* that will uniquely identify what you're looking for. It's better to use complete words and phrases instead of wildcards so that WordPerfect will find only the documents you're looking for.

But the opposite applies to filename searches. If you're searching for filenames in the File Pattern box, it's good to use wildcards because of DOS's restrictions on filenames (only eight characters plus a three-character extension). For example, you can find all the files that end in .doc just by entering *.doc.

### Build QuickFinder Indexes for Warp-Speed Searches

If you create QuickFinder indexes for the documents you search frequently, the QuickFinder will do incredibly fast searches. Once a document has been indexed, the QuickFinder has a record of *every word in it* in that index.

The QuickFinder doesn't come with any indexes prebuilt, because it doesn't know what's in your documents. The trick to using the Quick-Finder efficiently is to store documents of different types in directories of their own and then *index those directories.*

What should you index? Index files that are out of date—the kind you'd normally think of as being in long-term storage. After all, you can usually remember what's in the documents you've worked with recently.

For example, you might want to round up all the documents that are related to the Jones project you worked on last year and put them in a directory named C:\WPDOCS\JONES. Or bring together your collection of 1993 business letters and put them in a directory named C:\WPDOCS\93LTRS.

### Creating a QuickFinder Index

To create a QuickFinder index, click the QuickFinder button in a file management dialog box; then click Indexer. Choose Create and enter a descriptive name for the index, one that helps you recall what kind of documents have been indexed, such as Personal Letters 1993 or Monthly Reports Aug–Sept. You'll see the Create Index dialog box (Figure 5.22). Click Browse and highlight directories and specific files you want to include in that index. Click Add to add them one at a time. Click on [..] in the Directories box to go up one level of directories. When all the directories you want to include in that index are listed, click Generate and wait a while as QuickFinder builds the index.

### Using a QuickFinder Index

Using a QuickFinder index is pretty straightforward: When you use the QuickFinder, click the Search In button and choose QuickFinder Index; then pick the index you want to search in.

The real trick to using a QuickFinder index is to use those *logical operators* listed in Table 5.1 to narrow your searches so that you can easily locate the exact documents you want. Say that you want to find a

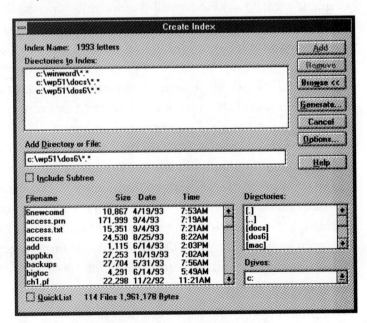

**Figure 5.22**  Choosing directories to index

document that you know has the word *random* in it, but that lots of your documents have that word in them. Try to think of another word that might be in only a few of the documents that also contain the word *random*. Say that word is *access*.

First, enter **random** in the QuickFinder's Search For box. Then type an ampersand (**&**) and enter **access** (Figure 5.23). Finally, choose OK. This will search for all documents containing both the word *random* and the word *access*.

---

## Don't Create One Index for a Whole Hard Disk!

You'll defeat the purpose of the QuickFinder if you think it's a shortcut to index all the documents on your hard disk using one index. Make smaller indexes for *classes* of documents and give those indexes descriptive names so that you can remember what they're for—like Jones Project Documents or 1993 Business Letters.

---

### QuickFinder Indexes All Kinds of Documents

WordPerfect's QuickFinder can index documents that were created in WordPerfect 4.2, 5.0, 5.1, 5.2, and 6.0. It can also index ASCII (DOS text) files.

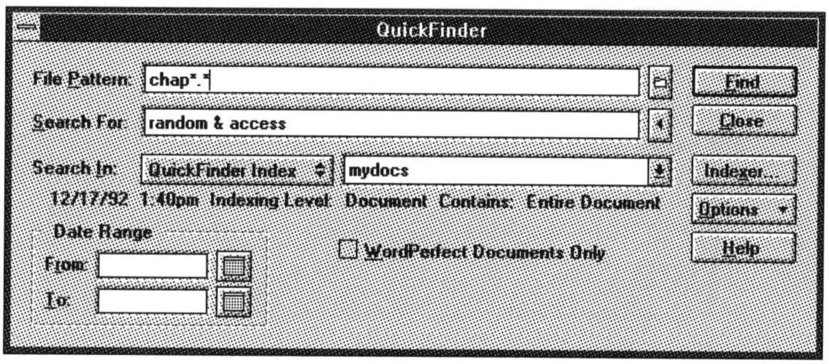

**Figure 5.23**   Searching for *random* and *access*

# Making Backups

WordPerfect 6.0 lets you make two different kinds of backups—timed document backups and original document backups. But, as you'll see from the next tricks, what you may think of as a backup often isn't a backup after all.

### TIP

### *Change the Time between Backups*

WordPerfect 6.0 comes with factory settings that make an automatic "backup" every 10 minutes (Figure 5.24). But if power goes out frequently where you live, set a shorter interval between timed document backups. I set mine for five minutes, which is about all I can remember of what I've typed. To change the time between backups, choose **P**references from the **F**ile menu or click the Files button in the Preferences button bar; then click Documents.

### TIP

### *Really Messed Up a Document? Recover Your Backup.*

The timed backups that WordPerfect 6.0 creates are stored in files named WP{WPC}.BK#, where # is the number of the document window the

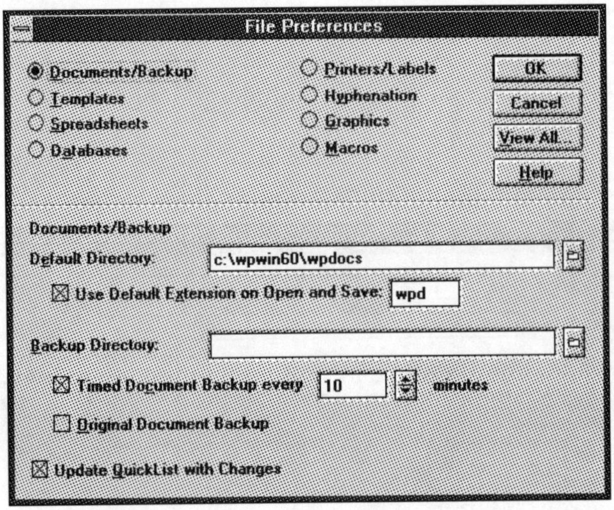

**Figure 5.24**  Setting the minutes between "backups"

document is in. Armed with this knowledge, here's a tip for getting editing changes back, even if you haven't saved a document.

Say you've made a bunch of changes without saving, but you decide that the last few changes have really messed things up. Instead of abandoning all your changes by exiting the document and getting the last-saved version back, open the timed backup file. (It will be located in whatever directory is listed for backup files in the Setup dialog box.) Check it; you may find most of the changes you want to keep.

---

### Document Backups Aren't Really Backups

 Don't be misled into thinking that you don't have to do backups because WordPerfect has a backup feature. The "backup" files the program makes are just duplicates of what you've been working on. If the power goes out, the next time you start WordPerfect you'll see a dialog box asking whether you want to open, rename, or delete the backup files of the documents you were working on. All these backup files are named WP{WP}.BK#, where # represents the number of the document window that the document in question was in. If you think that the backup is more recent than your last-saved version, open it, compare it to the last-saved version, and if it's more recent, save it with the same name as the version you last saved. If it's not more up to date, close it without saving it. Or choose Rename and give it a name that lets you know it's a copy so that you can check it later. If you choose Delete, though, it's gone for good.

But if your hard disk crashes and you haven't made backups (copies on a separate disk stored preferably in another location), those "automatic backups" will go down with the disk. So make backups on floppy disks or backup tape drives of the work you want to keep. See the upcoming sidebar "Safe Saves."

## Safe Saves

The timed document backups and original document backups that WordPerfect makes aren't really backups; they're just duplicates of your work. It's a great idea to use these features, but if your hard disk crashes and you haven't made copies on a separate disk, you've still lost your work. Real backups are stored on a different medium—such as on a floppy disk or a tape drive. For belt-and-suspenders protection, store these copies away from your usual work area in case of fire or your typical local disaster (earthquakes, where I live).

Original document backups are duplicates of the previous version of a document. Think of them as the parent generation of the child version you're saving now. That's the version that's usually overwritten when you save a document under the same name.

If you choose to use original document backups, WordPerfect makes a duplicate of the previous version of your document with the extension .BK! every time you save a document. So, you can get that previous version back if you have to. If that's important for the kind of work you do, turn on this feature, because it's normally off.

By the way, original document backups aren't really backups, either. The same warning about hard disk crashes applies here, too.

## Get Rid of Old .BK! Files

If you've turned on the Original Document Backup feature, be warned that old .BK! files will multiply like coathangers as the program saves an additional copy of each document every time you save it. Make a habit of deleting outdated .BK! files every so often. If you really want belt-and-suspenders protection, move those files to floppies, but get them off your hard disk soon.

# Using Document Summaries

Document summaries are an additional feature of WordPerfect that lets you keep track of the documents you create. Once you've started using document summaries, you can locate documents by keywords; by subjects or types that you assign to them; according to the author and typist of the document; or by date of creation or revision.

To assign a document summary, open the document first. You can't create a document summary for a document that's not on the screen. Then choose Document Summary from the **F**ile menu and fill out the dialog box (Figure 5.25) with as much or as little information as you want to keep track of.

Remember to save your document with its new summary, even if you haven't changed the text of the document itself.

## *Turning Off Document Summaries*

 Each time you open a document, WordPerfect scans your document summaries. This can slow things down quite a bit when you're in a hurry. The manual doesn't tell you how to stop the document summary scans. Here's how: Press **Ctrl+O**, click Setup, and choose Filename Only next to Show under File List Display.

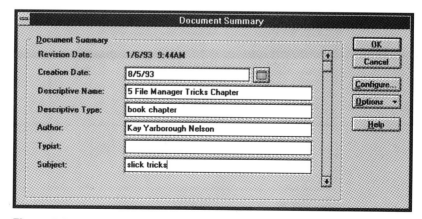

**Figure 5.25**   Setting up a document summary

### Save Document Summaries Separately from the Document

Some people in big offices like to save their document summaries as separate files. Click the Options button in the Document Summary dialog box if you want to do that.

### Print Out Document Summaries, Too

If you work in an office managing word-processing documents, you may also keep a big binder of document summaries on file. You can print a document summary from the Document Summary dialog box or from the Print dialog box.

### Customize Your Document Summaries

You can set up document summaries to use the information you choose for them. Click the Configure button while you're looking at the Document Summary dialog box. Then add whatever fields you want from the Document Summary Configuration dialog box (Figure 5.26). Key words are handy to add if you're going to be managing a huge volume of documents.

### Using Abstracts

You can either type an abstract, or summary of what a document contains, or you can have WordPerfect extract the first 40 lines of text in your document and use it as the abstract. In a letter, that will include all the name and address information, the salutation, and the

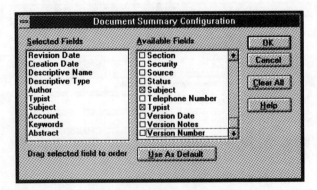

**Figure 5.26**  Custom-tailoring a document summary

first paragraph. Typing an abstract for each document can be time-consuming, so use the Extract feature and let WordPerfect do the work. Just click Options and choose Extract Information from Document.

### Protect Your Documents with Passwords

If there are some documents you want to keep others out of, you can assign them a password to stop folks from opening them. No one will be able to look at, print, or delete a password-protected document *within WordPerfect.* However, anybody can delete that document at the DOS prompt or in the Windows File Manager, so it's not really "protected," just locked. Still, some protection is better than none if you need it.

To assign a password to a document, choose Save **As** from the **File** menu. Enter a name for the document; then check Password Protect. Type the password you want to use and choose OK. You'll have to retype it so that the program can confirm it, just in case you made a mistake typing it the first time.

### If You Forget Your Password, You're in Trouble

WordPerfect encrypts the password you enter and stores it invisibly with the document. All the backup files, undelete files, and so forth that are associated with that document are locked, too. WordPerfect Corporation will *not* help you get your password back. Just use the *same password* for all your documents, and you'll stand less chance of forgetting it.

### Capitalization Doesn't Count in WordPerfect Passwords

Although it does matter to some programs whether you use capital or lowercase letters in a password, WordPerfect doesn't care. It will recognize SMOKEY or smokey or smoKEY as your password.

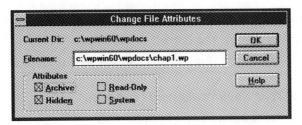

**Figure 5.27**   Protecting a file by changing its
attributes

### *Really Want to Protect a File? Don't Use a Password in WordPerfect.*

There are a couple of other much sneakier things you can do to protect
your files. You can change a file's attributes and make it read-only so
that it can't be changed, or make it hidden so that it doesn't show up
in any directory listing. To do this, click the File Options button in a
file management dialog box, choose Change Attributes, enter the file's
path name, and click the Read Only or Hidden box and OK (Figure
5.27).

If you make files hidden, better keep a list of their names, because
they won't show up in directory listings until you uncheck the Hidden
box. You can still work with them, though. To open a hidden file, just
enter its name in the Filename box in an Open dialog box. To display a
hidden file's name again, enter its path name in the Change Attributes
dialog box, keeping the Hidden box unchecked, and click OK.

# What Next?

In this chapter, you've seen all kinds of tricks for managing your documents through WordPerfect. In the next chapter, we'll look at slick
tricks that almost everyone can use, because they're about printing.

# Chapter 6

· · · · · · · · · · · · · · · · · · · · · · ·

## Printing Tricks

IT SEEMS LIKE IF ANYTHING goes wrong anywhere, it goes wrong with printing! Yet, we usually depend on having paper copies of almost all our documents, so this chapter will give you some slick tricks to use when printing. Although there are way too many printers available to list them by make and model, you'll find tricks in this chapter you can use with all different kinds of printers.

### Goodbye, Print Preview

The Print Preview feature you may be used to from earlier versions of WordPerfect is gone. To see how your document looks when printed, click the Page Zoom Full button on the power bar. It's on the far right, the one with the magnifying-glass icon.

### The Print Shortcut Key: F5

Pressing **F5** is the same as choosing **P**rint from the **F**ile menu. It takes you to the Print dialog box (Figure 6.1), where you can choose which pages to print, how many copies, and so forth.

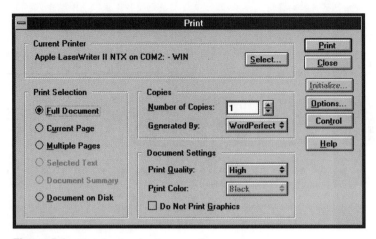

**Figure 6.1** Setting printing options

### *Shortcut to Printing: Ctrl+P*

If what you want is one copy of the document that's on your screen, press **Ctrl+P** to bypass the Print dialog box.

### *Print Only the Pages You Want*

You can print just a few pages instead of printing a complete document. This can really save a few trees, and it's faster than printing 50 pages you don't want just to get the five or so you do want.

To print selected pages, choose **M**ultiple Pages and then click Print in the Print dialog box. You'll see the dialog box in Figure 6.2.

Next to Page(s), enter the page numbers you want to print, using the following system:

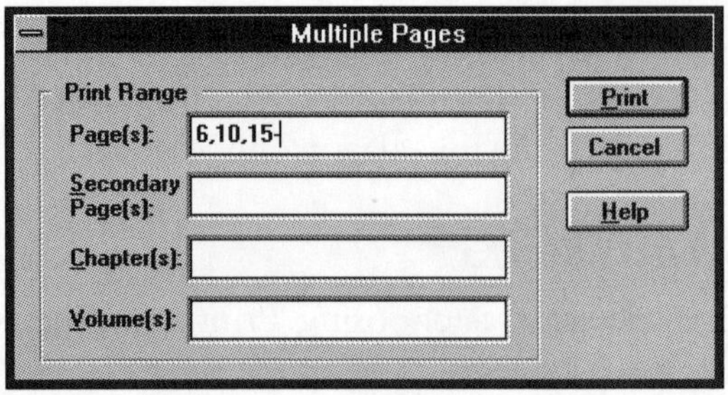

**Figure 6.2** Printing selected pages

♦ Separate single page numbers by commas. For example, if you wanted to print pages 28, 85, and 92, you'd enter **28, 85, 92**. You can omit the commas, but it's safer to include them so that you can see any mistake you make, such as typing 1 2 when you meant to type 12.

♦ Use a dash to indicate "to the end (or beginning) of the document." For example, to print from page 15 to the end of the document, enter **15–**. To print from the first page through page 15, enter **–15**.

♦ Use a dash to specify a range of pages to print. For example, to print pages 5 through 10, enter **5–10**.

You can combine all this shorthand to specify several different parts at once. For example, entering **1, 5, 10–15, 25–** will print page 1, page 5, pages 10 through 15, and from page 25 to the end of the document.

### Enter Pages You Want to Print in Numerical Order

If you're entering several page numbers, be sure to list them in numerical order or you'll get only the first page. WordPerfect reads them in numerical order, so if you enter something like 21–27, 8, you'll get only pages 21 through 27.

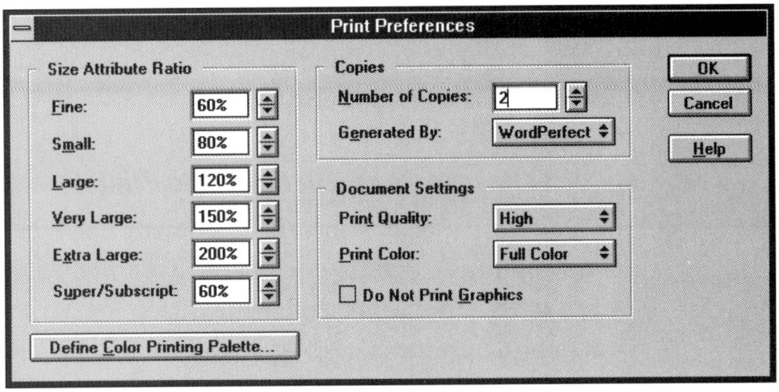

**Figure 6.3** Setting print preferences

### Reset the Default Number of Copies

If you almost always want two (or more) copies of everything you print, just set the default number of copies to print to 2 (or more). Click the Printer button on the Preferences button bar. You'll see the dialog box in Figure 6.3.

### Print Odd and Even Pages

WordPerfect normally prints all the pages you specify, but you can tell it to print just the odd (right-hand) pages or just the even (left-hand) pages. If your printer can print on only one side of the paper at a time, you can use this trick to print documents on both sides of the sheet: Print all the odd pages first; then put the printed pages back into the printer with the blank side ready to print and print the even pages.

Click the Options button in the Print dialog box; then choose Odd from the pop-up list next to Print Odd/Even pages. When they're printed, put them back face down in the paper tray and print the even pages. Normally, you'll want the last page on top, face down. (If that last page of the document is odd-numbered, take it out of the stack, because nothing's supposed to be printed on the back of it.) This time, choose Print In Reverse Order (Back To Front from the Print Output Options dialog box.

Depending on how your printer sends paper to its output tray, you may have to rearrange the pages. Best suggestion: Test-print a few pages and see what your printer does before you print an entire document or half of one.

If you're printing a document that's going to be bound, see the trick "WordPerfect Adjusts Gutter Space for Two-Sided Printing of Bound Documents" later in this chapter.

### You Don't Have to Open a Document to Print It

WordPerfect normally prints the document that's being displayed in the active window. To print a document that's *not* being displayed on your screen, open any file management dialog box, choose the file(s) you want to print, and then right-click on the file list and choose Print.

## Nothing Happening at Your Printer?

Depending on whether you're printing with a WordPerfect printer or a Windows printer, you can check to see what's going on with the printing process with this trick: Press **Ctrl+Esc** and choose Print Manager or WordPerfect Print Job, depending on which one's listed.

### Check On the Printing Process

There are several different ways to check on what's going on at your printer as a document's being printed:

♦ Press **F5** or click the Print button on the power bar and click the Control button.

♦ Click the document's Minimize button, and the Print Process icon (or the Print Manager icon, depending on whether you're using a WordPerfect printer or a Windows printer) will appear. Double-click on it.

♦ Hold down the **Alt** key and press **Tab** until you see WP Print Process or Print Manager.

### Stopping Printing

Sometimes it's useful to pause the printer while you find the laser labels, for example, or run around looking for a new box of letterhead. To stop (pause) printing from the Windows Print Manager, choose Pause. This temporarily suspends printing until you choose Resume.

To stop printing everything in a hurry, double-click the Print Manager's Close box. This cancels all the printing in progress.

### Rushing a Print Job

It's noon, and they're waiting for you in the hall. But you've got to get one letter out before you can leave. You can jump that document to the head of the print queue with this slick trick.

In the Print Manager, just drag the icon of any document (other than the one that's being printed right now) to a new place on the list.

## Printing a Section of Text May Result in Strange Spacing

When you select text and then choose Print, WordPerfect automatically chooses Selected Text in the Print dialog box and prints just that selection. The trap is that it will be printed on the page at the place where the text would normally fall *if you had printed the whole page*. So, for example, if you're printing the last paragraph on a page, you'll get a lot of blank space above it, or if you're printing a selection that occurs at the bottom of one page and the top of the next page, you'll get two pages, both with lots of blank space on them.

To get around this trap, copy the text you want to print into a new document window and then print.

### Get Collated Copies When WordPerfect Generates Printed Documents

You'll see in the Print dialog box a "Generated By" choice under Number of Copies. If you're printing several copies of a long document, leave it set to WordPerfect so that your copies will be collated. If you choose Printer, your copies may be printed a little faster, but you'll have to collate them by hand, separating all the Page 1s, Page 2s, and so on.

### View Facing Pages to Check for Balance

If you're printing two-sided pages, or if you're sending a document out to be printed and bound, by all means choose Two Page from the View menu and check your double-page spreads for balance. You may not want a right-hand (odd-numbered) page with only a few lines of text on it, because when the reader opens the book, a mostly blank page on the right looks like a mistake. If this occurs, some judicious editing may be in order.

Remember, you can use features like Conditional End of Page and Block Protect (see Chapter 3) to prevent text and graphics from being split between pages.

### *WordPerfect Adjusts Gutter Space for Two-Sided Printing of Bound Documents*

The gutter is the space between the left margin (on right-hand pages) or right margin (on left-hand pages) and the edge of the paper—in other words, it's that strip down the middle of the book that pages disappear into. If text is too close to that binding, you won't be able to read it. Fortunately, WordPerfect can adjust these margins automatically.

If a document's going to be printed and bound, do this to add binding space before you send it out or print it yourself:

**1** Open the document.

**2** Choose **P**age from the **L**ayout menu; then choose **B**inding.

**3** Select the edge the document will be bound on.

**4** Enter a measurement for the amount of extra space to add to the inside margin, say 0.25˝. This amount will be added only in the printed document, but keep in mind that if you add space to one margin and you want to keep the same amount of space in the outside margins, you should adjust the text margins to compensate. Paper, after all, does come in fixed sizes.

**5** If your printer prints on both sides of the page (like a LaserJet IIID), pick one of the Duplexing options.

You can see the binding width area if you look at Page or Two-Page view; it will appear with a crosshatch pattern.

If your document's not being printed on *both sides of the paper*, forget this trick. What you want to do is adjust the left margin (see Chapter 3).

### *Don't Print Graphics if You're Proofing a Document*

Graphics are very slow to print. If you're proofing the text of a document, turn off graphics printing to speed up things. Check the Do Not Print Graphics box in the Print dialog box.

### *Print to a File to Print* without *WordPerfect!*

If you use this slick trick, you can print a WordPerfect document on a computer that isn't even running WordPerfect—or Windows, for that matter. It's called *printing to a file* or *printing to disk*. You can just take the resulting file on a floppy disk to any computer that's running DOS and print your document without using WordPerfect at all. There are two catches: First, you'll need to install the printer you plan to print the document on, even though it's not connected to your machine. Second, the procedure as described in this trick works on WordPerfect printers. You can do the same thing with a Windows printer, but the dialog boxes you'll see are slightly different.

**1** With the document you want to print later on the screen, choose **S**elect Printer from the **F**ile menu.

**2** Highlight the printer you ultimately plan to print the document on.

**3** Choose **S**etup.

**4** For a Destination, choose **P**ort.

**5** Choose Prompt for Filename so that you can rename the file each time you use this "printer."

**6** In the Filename box, type **a:\** or **b:\**, depending on whether you're going to use drive A or B as the drive for the floppy disk that the file's going to. (It's a good idea to put a disk *in* that drive about now, too.)

**7** Type a name for the document—for example **mydoc.txt**, so that the line looks like this for a disk in drive A: **a:\mydoc.txt**.

**8** In the Select Printer dialog box, make sure that the printer you just set up is selected.

**9** In the Print dialog box, choose **F**ull Document and **P**rint.

That's it. You've created a file named MYDOC.TXT that you can take on the floppy disk over to another computer that's not running WordPerfect, and print it from the DOS prompt. Better go back now and select your regular printer so that the one that's not connected doesn't stay selected.

When you get to the other computer, assuming the floppy disk with the file on it is in drive A, at the DOS prompt, type **copy a:\mydoc.txt /b prn**. This will print the document on the printer that's connected to the first parallel port on the other computer. If it's on a different port there, use LPT2, LPT3, COM1, COM2, or COM3 for whatever port it's on. (How will you know? Try until it prints. Beats looking in the backs of these things.)

Don't try to print a document that's been saved to disk from within WordPerfect. Print it from the DOS prompt.

## Tricks for Envelopes and Mailing Labels

One of the most frustrating printing jobs is trying to get envelopes and mailing labels to print right. Use the tricks in this section to speed up these chores.

### *Change Fonts for Envelope Text*

You aren't restricted to using the same font on envelopes that you're using in the document. Go right ahead and click the Font button in the Envelope dialog box and format your addresses however you want. Use a different font for the return address and the mailing address if you like. You can use WordPerfect's special characters, too: Just press **Ctrl+W** and insert them.

---

**Omit the Return Address on Preprinted Envelopes**

You don't want a return address printed over your printed return address in the upper left corner of your expensive envelopes. If you normally use those, uncheck the Print Return Address box in the Envelope dialog box (Figure 6.4).

---

### *A POSTNET Bar Code on Envelopes Speeds Up Mailing*

If you know the 9-digit ZIP code for the address you're mailing to, you can speed up delivery of your letter by having WordPerfect put the bar code on the letter. If you know only the 5-digit ZIP code, don't bother: That won't speed up your letter and in some cases may actually slow it down, because the post office may obliterate the bar code!

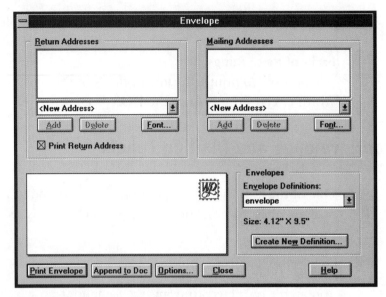

**Figure 6.4** Setting up an envelope

But getting the 9- or 11-digit bar code can help that letter make the next plane, so use it. All you need to do is click the Options button and then check the Include USPS POSTNET Bar Code box.

### Get the Right Mailing Address on the Envelope

WordPerfect looks for a section of left-aligned text that ends with a ZIP code followed by two hard returns and automatically puts it in the Mailing Addresses part of the Envelope dialog box. If you have several addresses in your letter, the program may not guess the right one. To avoid this and make sure the address you want to use as the mailing address gets used, highlight it before you click the Envelope button on the WordPerfect button bar.

### Save the Envelope with Your Letter

If you always print an envelope each time you print a letter, let WordPerfect keep track of the envelope for you. After you've filled out the Envelope dialog box, click the Append to Doc button. Now when you print the letter, the envelope will be printed immediately after.

### Speedy Envelope Printing

Here's one way to speed up printing envelopes by printing a batch of them at the same time. Open a new document and type the addresses for the envelopes, separating each one with two hard returns. Now create envelopes for each address, highlighting each one first so that Word-Perfect will use it as the mailing address. Choose Append To Doc for each one. Now you can print the whole document and you'll get one envelope after another. Save the document so that you can use it again.

### Printing Envelopes Correctly

The best thing to do is see how your envelopes come out by test printing them on paper, instead of using actual envelopes. That way, if you guess wrong and text shows up where you don't expect it, you'll still see it. If you use an envelope to test-print, the text may get printed on your printer's platen, where there is no envelope. And you don't want that, because the ink will stay there and may come off on other documents.

My advice is once you get an envelope printing right, stick one on your wall in exactly the right orientation for your envelope feeder (if you have one). If it goes through face up, sketch the flap on the front (and mark it "back side") so that you'll feed it into the feeder exactly right. This simple trick has saved me printing many an envelope again.

---

### Press Ctrl+Enter between Mailing Labels

This has to be the most often overlooked trap when you print mailing labels from a document that consists of addresses (instead of doing a mail merge). To WordPerfect, each label is a tiny "page," and it needs a page break between it and the next label. The addresses look all right to you on the screen, but you wind up getting *one label per sheet*. That's not what you want. Press **Ctrl+Enter** between each address.

---

### Setting Up a Custom Label Format

The real trick is: don't. Buy 3M or Avery labels that come in standard sizes. WordPerfect is already set up to use these sizes on any printer you can print on. It's a hassle measuring labels exactly, including the distance between columns and rows, the distance between the top edge of the sheet and the first label, and so forth. This is a slick tricks book. Buy standard labels.

### Display Labels Only for Your Type of Printer

WordPerfect is set up to display all the mailing label formats available. The ones for tractor-fed and laser printers are very different, and if you have one kind of printer and not the other, it's going to be much easier to find the label format you want to use if you display the ones just for the type of printer you have. Click the Tractor-Fed or Laser buttons at the top of the Labels dialog box (Figure 6.5).

### Test-Print a Label Sheet on Plain Paper

To avoid wasting expensive laser labels, test-print one sheet on paper. Then hold it up to the light with a real label sheet behind it to make sure lines of text aren't getting cut off in the middle.

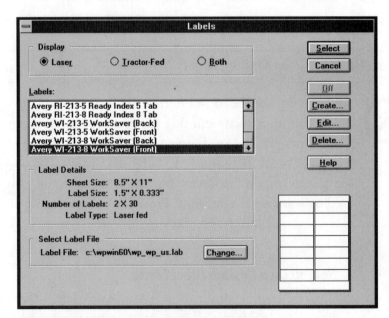

**Figure 6.5**  Displaying only laser labels

### Centering Text on Labels

To center text on labels, just press **Ctrl+E** at the beginning of your document. To center labels vertically, too, choose Page from the Layout menu; then pick Center and choose Current and Subsequent pages.

### Print a Whole Sheet of Labels with Each New Project

Every time I start a project, I print out a whole sheet of mailing labels for the address or addresses that are going to be involved. Saves a lot of time later. Just copy the first address and paste it in the document as many times as you have label spaces on your sheet. Press **Ctrl+Enter** to insert a page break between each label.

## Tricks for Printing Troubles

Sometimes your printer just won't print. If that happens, try any or all of these slick tricks to find out where the problem lies.

### Try Printing from DOS As a Test

If your printer won't print from the DOS prompt, there's something wrong outside WordPerfect and Windows. It's fairly easy to test to see if this is the case.

First, look at the cable that's connecting your printer and computer to see if it's connected to a COM (serial) port or an LPT (parallel) port. If the cable connector has sockets at the computer end, it's most likely connected to a COM port, usually COM1; if it has pins, it's probably connected to LPT1.

Once you've figured out which port your printer's on, go to the DOS prompt. Then type copy con lpt1 (if it's on an LPT port) or copy con com1 (if it's on a COM port). Press **Enter**. Then type testing and press **Enter**. Now:

♦ If your printer isn't a laser printer, press **Ctrl+z**.

♦ If your printer is a laser printer but isn't a PostScript printer, press **Ctrl+l**, then **Enter**, and then **Ctrl+z**.

The printer should print out a page with the word *testing* on it.

If you have a Postscript laser printer, such as an Apple LaserWriter NTX, the routine is slightly different. Type **showpage** instead of **testing**. Then press **Ctrl+d**, **Enter**, **Ctrl+z**, and **Enter**. You should get a blank page.

If nothing happens when you try this test of printing from DOS, the problem isn't in WordPerfect but most likely is in your printer.

---

### Getting Gibberish with the Wrong Printer

Sometimes your printer spits out garbage. The most common reason for this is that you've selected a printer in WordPerfect other than the one you're really using. Choose Select Printer from the File menu and pick the right one.

### Getting the Wrong Fonts

The most common cause of this trouble is that you've selected a different printer than the one you originally set up the document for, and that second printer doesn't support the font you're asking for. Check to see which printer's selected.

---

# Font Tricks

WordPerfect lets you manipulate fonts in all kinds of ways that may not have occurred to you. Use the tricks in this section for some very sophisticated fine-tuning.

### Picking an Initial Font

The *initial font* is the font that's automatically used whenever you start a new document in WordPerfect. Each printer you install can have a different initial font. So if you select a different printer, don't be surprised to see the screen change.

To change to a different initial font, press **F9** or **Ctrl+F** to open the Font dialog box and click Initial Font. Pick the font you want and click OK. This will change the font used in the document that's on the

## More than You Want to Know about Fonts

There are two kinds of fonts: *printer fonts* and *screen fonts*. You need to understand the basic difference between them. Printer fonts are the characters your printer prints, and screen fonts (your manual also calls these graphics fonts) are the characters you see on the screen. When you're looking at the screen, the fonts you see aren't exactly what you're going to get when you print, for one very obvious reason: The screen isn't the size of a sheet of paper.

WordPerfect uses a set of basic screen fonts to display the closest match to the printer font you've selected. You can install additional screen (graphics) fonts as well as additional printer fonts—that is, if your printer will accept new fonts. Most dot-matrix printers won't.

Why should you have to install fonts at all? Maybe you don't. When you install a printer, WordPerfect automatically recognizes the fonts that come with it, which are called the printer's built-in fonts. However, if you acquire more fonts later, you'll need to tell the program which fonts you've bought and where they're stored. Some printers accept new fonts on disk (soft fonts), and some printers use cartridge fonts. First, you'll need to install them according to the documentation that comes with them. Then you'll need to install them *in WordPerfect* by choosing Select Printer from the File menu and then choosing Setup. This last step is the one that's most often overlooked.

Now, this topic is a little advanced for this book, but if you're having font troubles, you need to know just a tiny bit about what goes on behind the scenes. So, here goes. WordPerfect keeps information about all the prints it supports in an .ALL file. When you install a printer, it creates a specific .PRS (printer resource) file for that printer. Printer fonts are kept in .ALL files, too. HP fonts, for example, are kept in a WPHP1.ALL file. When you install a printer font, it's copied to your particular printer's .PRS file. This is why it's very important to select the right printer before you install fonts.

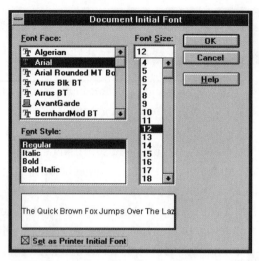

**Figure 6.6**   **Changing to a different initial font**

screen. Be sure to check the Set as Printer Initial Font (Figure 6.6) if you want that font to be the one used in all your new documents from now on.

### Change Which Screen Fonts WordPerfect Uses

Press **F9** and click Font Map. You'll see a complex dialog box. Click Display, and you'll see which screen font WordPerfect is using (on the

**Measuring Type Sizes**   WordPerfect measures fonts two ways—in points ($\frac{1}{72}$ of an inch) and in characters per inch, or cpi. The measurement that's used depends on the kind of printer you've got. Dot-matrix printers usually use cpi, and laser or inkjet printers use points. Now, points is a vertical measurement (height) and cpi is a horizontal measurement (width). A 10-point font is 10 points high (roughly, for you purists out there) and a 12-point size in the same font is bigger. It works the opposite for cpi: a bigger number means a smaller font. Think about it. If you squeeze 12 characters per inch into the same space as 10 characters per inch, they're going to be smaller. This distinction drove me crazy until I got used to it. If you switch between a dot-matrix printer for proofing output and a laser printer for final output, it can drive you crazy, too.

right) to display which printer font (on the left); (see Figure 6.7). Pick a different display font for that particular printer font if you like. It won't affect how your document is printed, only how you see it on the screen.

### Free Disk Space by Getting Rid of Some Fonts

WordPerfect comes with a lot of fonts, and so do many of the other Windows programs you bought. Fonts take up lots of space on your hard disk, so why not delete the ones you'll never use? Go to the Windows Control Panel, double-click the Fonts icon, and highlight each font. If you can live without it, Ctrl-click on it to mark it. When you've marked all the fonts you want to delete, click Remove, check the Delete Font from Disk box, and click on Yes to All.

### WordPerfect's Automatic Font Change Customizes Fonts

When you call for a particular text attribute, such as boldface or italics, or pick a relative font size, such as Large or Small, WordPerfect looks in a table of AFCs (Automatic Font Changes) to choose the actual font that will be used. If you don't like a particular italic or bold—you can change it! But there's a trap, too: The change you make works only with the printer that's currently selected because of the way WordPerfect handles printing.

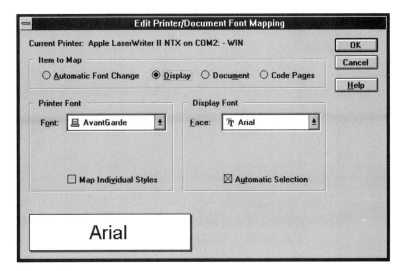

**Figure 6.7** Changing the display font

In the Font Map dialog box (see the trick "Change Which Screen Fonts WordPerfect Uses" earlier in this chapter), click Automatic Font Change. Click Map Individual styles to specify exactly what you want to be used for specific styles, such as italics. Pick the font you want to change. Under Automatic Font Change (Figure 6.8), choose the attribute you want to map, such as Very Large Print. Then pick the face, style, and size (on the right side of the dialog box) that you want WordPerfect to use.

Remember: This change is good *only* for the printer that's currently selected!

## Not Getting Your WP Characters?

If the WP Characters box comes up empty when you press **Ctrl+W**, it means that the WordPerfect TrueType fonts that come with the program weren't installed or were somehow deleted.

Double-click on the WP 6.0 Installation icon in your WordPerfect for Windows program group (or get the original installation disks out, put the Install 1 disk in your floppy drive, choose Run from the Program Manager's File menu, and enter a:install or b:install, depending on which drive the disk is in). Choose Custom and Files. Click the **WordPerfect Program box. Click OK and Begin Installation.

When you're done, you've installed all 1400+ WordPerfect characters. You may not want them all! Go to the Windows Control Panel, double-click on the Fonts icon, and scroll down to where the WP fonts live. You may have no need for characters like Cyrillic A & B (Russian). See the previous trick for how to remove them from your hard disk to make room for useful stuff.

### Changing the Relative Font Sizes

WordPerfect enlarges or reduces fonts by a certain percentage when you choose Extra Large, Very Large, or Small (under Relative Size in the Font dialog box). A slick trick: You can change these percentages so that Small is smaller or Large is larger. All you have to do is click the Printer icon on the Preferences button bar. Under Size Attribute ratio, you'll

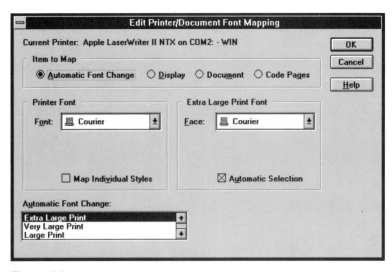

**Figure 6.8**  Mapping automatic font changes

see the percentages WordPerfect is using and you can change them (Figure 6.9).

## Now What?

· · · · · · · · · · · · · · · · · · · · · · · · · · · · · · · ·

Now that you've seen an awful lot of printing tricks, let's look at something that's more fun: all kinds of slick tricks that you can pull to make your life easier and your work smoother.

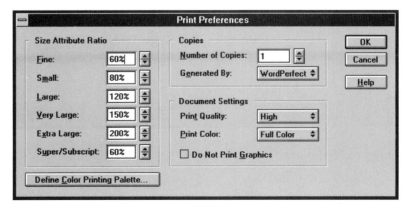

**Figure 6.9**  Changing a font's relative size

# Chapter 7

## All Sorts of Neat Tricks

O NE OF THE NEATEST THINGS ABOUT SLICK TRICKS is that they can make "advanced" parts of the program very accessible to you, without your having to learn all the fundamentals of an advanced feature. For example, WordPerfect 6.0 lets you create equations, embed sounds, insert graphics in your documents, and create macros. In addition, the program has lots of features that you may rarely use, such as collapsible outlining, tables of contents, indexing, tables of authorities, footnotes and endnotes, automatic reference lists, line numbering, and paragraph numbering, to name just some of them. You'll see slick tricks for these features in this chapter.

A lot of these are pretty sophisticated features, so don't expect to be taught all the ins and outs of them, or even the basics of them, here. But if a slick trick or two for an obscure (nor not-so-obscure) part of the program is what you want, look in this chapter.

## Tricks with Graphics

WordPerfect comes with a good-sized collection of graphics that you can use in your documents without knowing much about graphics at all.

Of course, if you want to get further into graphics, you can do some even fancier things after you spend some time with the manual. But the slick tricks in this section are ones just about anybody can use in any kind of document.

### Graphics That Come with WordPerfect

Before you start playing with graphics in your documents, it's a good idea to see what you've got to work with. To review the graphic image collection that comes with WordPerfect, press **Ctrl+O** for Open. Double-click Graphics Directory in your QuickList. Then choose the first graphic image and click View. Keep pressing the **Down arrow** key to see them all.

### Resizing a Graphic Image Quickly

When you click in a graphic to select it, you'll see little "knobs" appear around it. These are its sizing handles. If you drag the handles in the corners inward or outward, you'll change the size of the graphic.

Drag a graphic's top, side, or bottom handles to change the graphic's size *without* keeping its original proportions.

If you resize a graphic by mistake, choose Undo (**Ctrl+Z**).

### Editing a Graphic Image

When you right-click on a graphic image, you'll get a QuickMenu. Choose Image Tools. The Image Tools toolbox (Figure 7.1) lets you rotate, scale, crop, or flip the image. Or you can click the Image Edit button to go to WP Draw.

If WP Draw is what you want to begin with, you can choose Edit Figure from that QuickMenu to go straight to WP Draw, but usually the Image Tools will do what you want.

Test-print your special effects before you fall in love with them. Some printers can't rotate graphics, for example, because they can't switch from Portrait to Landscape on the same page.

### Shift+F11 to Edit a Graphics Box

There's a built-in shortcut for editing a graphics box: Select the box and press **Shift+F11**. Note that this trick is for editing a graphics box, not a graphic image.

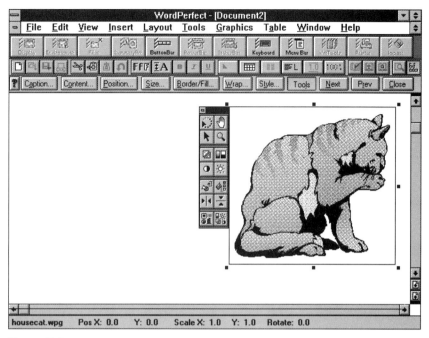

**Figure 7.1** Editing a graphic with the Image Tools toolbox

You'll see the Graphics Box feature bar in Figure 7.2.

### *Wrap Text Around the Shape of a Graphic Image*

Normally, WordPerfect wraps text around the rectangular graphics box that an image is contained in, but for a fancy effect in your document, you can have it wrap text around the *shape* of the image. To do this, right-click on the box and choose Wrap from the QuickMenu. There's also a Wrap button on the Graphics Box feature bar. You can then pick exactly how you want text to wrap (Figure 7.3).

### *Forcing a Graphic to Stay with Text*

Sometimes, you'll want a graphic image to always stay with a paragraph or even with a line of text. The trick here is to right-click on the box and then choose Position from the QuickMenu, or click the Position button on the Graphics Box feature bar. Then pick whether you want the box to stay with the paragraph or the character (Figure 7.4).

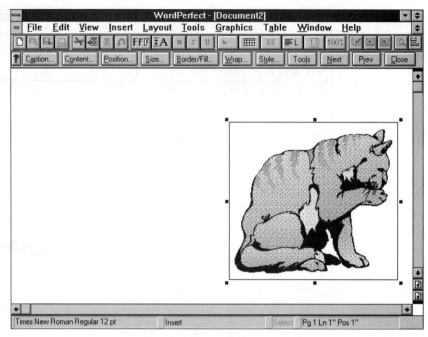

**Figure 7.2**    Displaying the Graphics Box feature bar

---

## A Graphics Box Attached to a Character Position May Produce Strange Effects

It may sound like a good idea to attach a graphic to a character position, because then you might think that the graphic will stay exactly where you want it. But WordPerfect will normally adjust the line height around a graphic image that you attach to a character position. So attach a graphic to a character only when the graphic is very small, like a symbol.

---

### Print Dot-Matrix Printer Color Graphics

Graphics (.WPG) files come in two classes: class 1 and class 2. Class 2 graphics, which come with WordPerfect 6.0, have shading in color areas; and class 1 graphics don't. If your dot-matrix printer can't print shading, you can convert the class 2 graphics to class 1.

Click the Figure button on the Graphics button bar and then double-click on the name of the graphic image you want. Then right-click the

**Figure 7.3** Choices for how you want text to wrap

graphic and choose Content. Choose Image on Disk from the Content pop-up list. As a final slick trick, change the name of the graphic by adding a 1 to the beginning of its name. This will tell you it's a class 1 graphic and will also put it at the top of your graphics list. Finally, from the drop-down format list, choose WordPerfect Graphics 1.0 and click OK.

### *Creating Reversed-Out Text*

Reversed-out text (white on black) is a very sophisticated touch if your printer can handle it. Most PostScript printers can. Test-print on your printer if you don't have a PostScript printer.

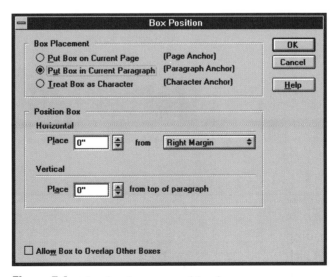

**Figure 7.4** Anchoring a graphics box

Here's one way to do it. Create a graphics box filled with 100% shading, set the text color to white, and type the text that you want to appear reversed out. (See Figure 7.5 for a sample.)

Before you start, click the Display button on the Preferences button bar and uncheck Show Windows System Colors so you can see the reversed-out text on your screen.

**1** Choose **C**ustom Box from the **G**raphics menu.

**2** Choose User as the style.

**3** Choose 100% Fill as the fill style, and click OK.

**4** Click the Content button and choose Text as the content, then click Edit.

**5** For the text, press **F9** and pick the font and size you want. Type the text; then move to the beginning of the text and set the text color to white (use the Color choice on the Font menu). If you set the color to white before you type, you won't be able to see your typing.

**6** Click OK and check the reversed-out text on your screen.

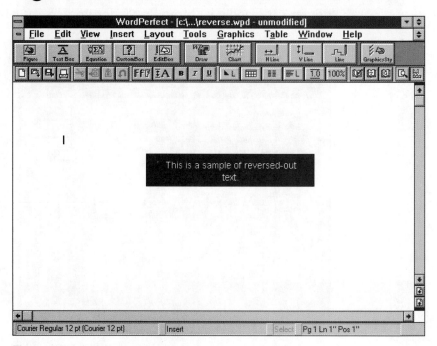

**Figure 7.5** **Reversing out text**

Now, test-print the reversed-out box on your printer to see if it can handle it. You may want to add a hairline border around the box to get sharp edges.

### Use the Reverse Macro

Now, here's the easy way to get reversed-out text: Play the Reverse macro that comes with WordPerfect. It reverses the text you've selected to white and puts it into a black graphics box.

Just select the text, press **Alt+F10**, enter reverse, and press **Enter**.

### Creating a Drop Cap

This one is easy, too. Play the Dropcap macro that comes with Word-Perfect 6.0. Don't bother getting out the manual. You can create a drop cap like the one in Figure 7.6.

You'll be prompted for the letter you want to use as the drop cap.

### Speeding Up WordPerfect and Graphics

Sometimes WordPerfect can slow way down because it has to redraw the screen often while you're editing a document with graphics in it. To

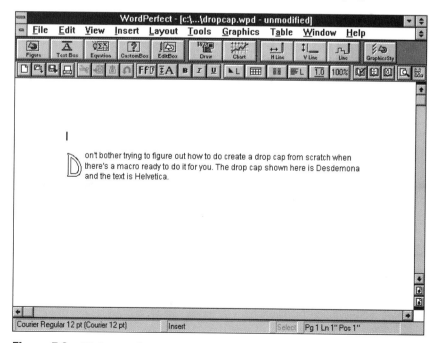

**Figure 7.6**  Using a drop cap

speed up the program, uncheck Graphics on the View menu so that graphic images won't be displayed as you edit. You'll just see empty graphics boxes instead.

### TextArt Creates Spectacular Text Effects

WP Draw is a separate program that comes with WordPerfect. It's excellent for editing graphic images and creating your own drawings from scratch. But for quick, spectacular effects in your documents, use TextArt instead. Click the TextArt button on the WordPerfect button bar, and enter the text for which you want to create special effects (Figure 7.7); you can use as many as 58 characters on three lines. Then go wild with the effects you can choose. Select a shape to which to conform text from the pallette of shapes to the right of the text box. Choose a different fill pattern, shadow effect, or rotation. This is an excellent way to create a custom letterhead.

### Putting Text in a Graphics Box

The easy way? Copy or cut the text; then paste it into a text box as you create the text box. Or right-click the box and choose Edit Text. If the box already contains a graphic image, you'll need to click the Content

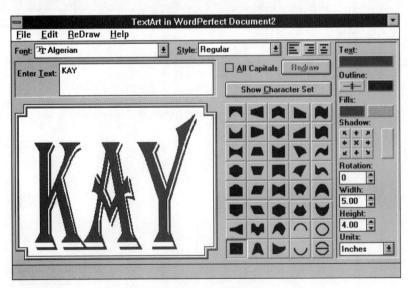

**Figure 7.7** Creating text effects in TextArt

button on the Graphics Box feature bar and tell WordPerfect that you want the box to contain text instead of graphics; then click Edit to enter the text.

### Mixing Text and Graphics

Have you ever wondered how to make use of all those fancy borders that come with WordPerfect? Here's the easy way to get text inside one of those graphic images (see Figure 7.8).

First, choose **F**igure from the **G**raphics menu and select the image you want to use. Then create a Custom box, choose User as the style, and click Content. Choose text as the content and click Edit. Now choose a font and size, type your text, and click OK. (You'll probably want to use center alignment if you're creating something to go inside one of the fancy borders.) Then, just drag the text box over the figure box. That's it.

Another way to mix text and graphics inside a graphics box is to use WP Draw. You can retrieve graphic images into WP Draw and add text to them.

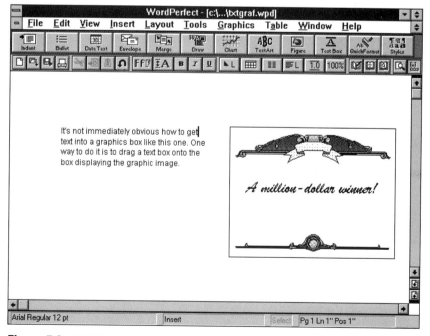

**Figure 7.8**  Mixing text and graphics

### Using Graphics Lines

One of the simplest but most effective ways you can use graphics in WordPerfect is to use horizontal and vertical lines. All you need to do is press **Ctrl+F11** for a horizontal line or **Ctrl+Shift+F11** for a vertical line. Then just drag the line to move it or resize it. To make a line larger or smaller, drag it by one of its handles.

### Create Charts Quickly from a Table

WordPerfect 6.0 can create very professional-looking charts from data in a table. Just put the cursor anywhere in the table and click the Chart button on the Tables button bar or the WordPerfect button bar. Instant charting!

WordPerfect 6.0 takes the labels for the X axis of the chart (the bottom) from the first row that's in your table, starting with column B. The labels for the Y axis (on the left side, going up) are taken from whatever's in column A in your table (Figure 7.9). After the basic chart is drawn, you can customize it however you like.

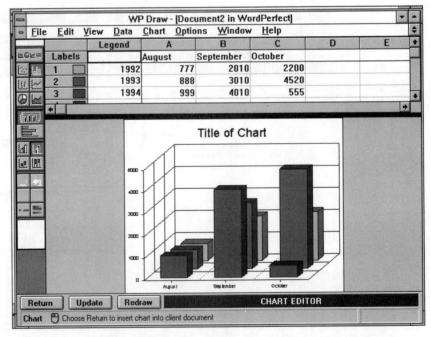

**Figure 7.9** A sample chart along with the table used to create it

# Easy Macro Tricks

Macros aren't hard. At least, not the "easy" kind of macro—the kind in which you turn on the macro recorder and WordPerfect simply records everything you do, including the mistakes you make and correct. You don't have to learn any special macro language or have any programming experience to use macros.

Macros are wonderful for the things you rarely do, because you have to do them only once. Then, you can forget about how you did them and just play the macro back. They're also wonderful for the things that you do all the time, every day, because they'll save you a lot of keystrokes and keep you from making mistakes. The tricks in this section will be mostly for these day-to-day macros.

Once you've recorded a macro, you can make it into a button. Once you have a button, you can carry out a task by just clicking on that button. What could be easier than that?

You can use macros for all sorts of things:

- ♦ Typing addresses that you use almost every day.
- ♦ Typing boilerplate letters or standard paragraphs.
- ♦ Creating your letterhead.
- ♦ Typing a distribution list.
- ♦ Retrieving a graphic you use often and setting the border and other options that you use with it.
- ♦ Creating a special symbol that you use a lot.
- ♦ Filling out a fax cover sheet.

These are just a few ideas. As you read the tricks that follow, you'll think of more that you can use in your own work.

### *Shortcuts to Record and Play Macros*

Instead of choosing Macro from the Tools menu and then choosing **R**ecord or **P**lay, use these shortcuts:

| | |
|---|---|
| **Ctrl+F10** | Start or stop recording a macro |
| **Alt+F10** | Choose a macro to play |

### WordPerfect Comes with Lots of Prerecorded Macros

You can use these prerecorded macros without knowing anything about macros at all! To see which macros were supplied with your release of WordPerfect (you may have a later release than this book was based on), choose Macros from the **H**elp menu and select Shipping Macros. Figure 7.10 shows the beginning of the list that came with the first release of version 6.0.

Some of these macros are really useful, and you've seen suggestions for putting them to work throughout this book.

### Use Ctrl+Shift Key Shortcuts As Macro Names

When you're asked for the name of the macro as you start to record a macro, press **Ctrl+Shift**+ and a letter or number instead of a name if you plan to use that macro a lot. That way, you can play the macro quickly just by pressing that key combination.

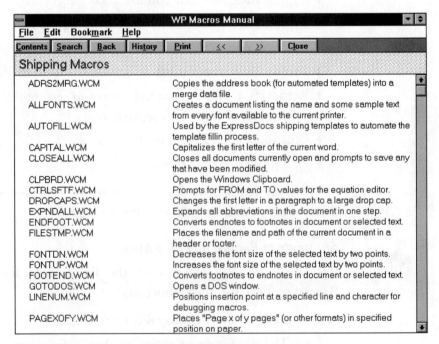

**Figure 7.10**   Macros supplied with WordPerfect

### *Assign a Favorite Macro to a Ctrl+Shift Key Combination*

You may not realize how much you're going to use a macro until you've used it for awhile. Then you'll want to assign it to a key combination. You can do that without rerecording the macro from scratch:

**1** Open a file management dialog box, such as the Open dialog box.

**2** Locate the directory that contains your macros.

**3** Select the macro you want to assign to a **Ctrl+Shift** key combination, click the File Options button, and choose Rename.

**4** Rename the macro **ctrlsft***n***.wpm** in the dialog box, where *n* represents the letter or number you want to assign to the macro. For example, to reassign a macro named memo.wcm to **Ctrl+Shift+M**, you'd rename it ctrlsftm.wcm.

---

### *Pressing Esc Doesn't Stop the Macro Recorder*

You might think that, since you can press **Esc** to get out of a dialog box or menu, you can also use it to get out of the macro recorder once it's rolling. Nope. Pressing **Esc** simply inserts an Esc keystroke into your macro. To stop recording a macro, press **Ctrl+F10**. (If you're in a dialog box, you'll usually need to exit it before you can stop the macro recorder.) Then rerecord the macro under the same name if you want to replace it, or edit it if you feel comfortable with editing macros (which we won't get into in this book).

---

### *Tricks for Recording Macros*

When you turn on the macro recorder, WordPerfect faithfully records everything you do. However, there are a few things you should be aware of before you spend a lot of trial-and-error time with the macro recorder:

♦ Record a macro under the conditions with which you expect to use it. If your macro is supposed to work in a blank document window, open a new document window before you turn on the macro recorder, or make opening that new document the first step in the macro. Or, if you're supposed to go to the beginning of a document so that a macro searches the entire document, do that before you record the macro, or have the keystrokes **Ctrl+Home** as the first step in the macro.

♦ Play a macro under the conditions it was recorded. For example, if you've recorded a macro that cuts or copies selected text, it won't do any good to play it until some text has been selected.

♦ Keep in mind that the macro recorder records only what you actually *do*. If you open menus without choosing anything from them as you're recording a macro, the macro recorder won't record anything. It records only what you actually select from menus and dialog boxes.

♦ Use the keyboard instead of the mouse if there's any chance of confusion. Any time you use the mouse in a document, you're recording a relative position in text. If the document on the screen isn't in exactly the same position as it was when you recorded the macro—which, say, selects some text—the text that gets selected when the macro plays may not be the same text that you intended.

Take your time as you record macros. The program will play them back faster than you can type, but there's no point in rushing as you record a macro.

### Repeating a Macro

Say that you've recorded a macro that inserts a special character, and you want to repeat that macro 20 times so that you'll get 20 of those special characters in your document. Choose Repeat from the **Edit** menu, enter the number of times (**20** in this case) you want the macro to repeat, and choose OK. Now play the macro and it will repeat 20 times, or as many times as you specified.

### Quickly Replaying a Macro

WordPerfect keeps track of the last macro you played, and it's easy to repeat it just by choosing it from the list on the Macro menu.

### Adding Macros to the List on the Menu

You can add nine more macros to the list on the Macro menu. Press **Alt+F10** and click the Menu button. Click Insert; then press **Alt+ Down arrow**. Choose the macro you want listed on the menu; pick Select and OK. Then choose Select and OK again, and it will be listed on the Macro menu.

## Tricks for Using the Speller

Don't overlook WordPerfect's Speller! It's wonderful for catching your typing mistakes. The Speller is the most basic writing tool of the three WordPerfect provides.

Make it a habit to spell-check each document before you print it, and you'll save many a tree.

### Save Documents before and after a Spell Check

This is the fundamental Speller trick. Save your document before you spell-check it and, more important, after you've spell-checked it. If you don't, all your changes will be lost and you'll have to spell-check it again.

### Use Ctrl+F1 to Start the Speller

This handy keyboard shortcut can save you from mousing around. **Ctrl+F2** starts the Speller, and **Alt+F1** starts the Thesaurus.

### When the Speller Can't Find Any Misspelled Words

Sometimes, you may ask the Speller to check the spelling of a particular word—and nothing happens, except you get a "Word Found" message. That means the word is spelled correctly.

### Look Up Word Patterns

This is a great tip to use when playing Scrabble and you can sneak out to your computer. In the Speller, type the word pattern in the Replace With box. Use the wildcards **?** to stand for any one character and **\*** to stand for any combination of characters, or no character at all. Say you want to check the spelling of *relieve* because you don't know whether it's ie or ei. You can enter rel*ve and then click Suggest to get a list of words like *relative, relieve,* and *relive.*

### Copy from the Speller to Your Document

Say you've looked up a word. Rather than run the risk of mistyping it again, just copy and paste it into your document. Highlight the word in the list that the Speller has found; then double-click on it in the Replace With box, press **Ctrl+C**, click twice in the document where you want the word to appear, and press **Ctrl+V**. Takes longer to explain than to do.

### Turn Off Checking for Numbers in Words

If your work requires you to type lots of letter-number combinations, such as F1 and A256, tell the Speller not to bother you about combinations like this. Choose Options from the Speller menu and uncheck the Words With **N**umbers option.

### WordPerfect Checks for Irregular Capitalization

If the Speller runs across a word that's capitalized irregularly, such as OnCe, it will stop and query you on it. You can turn off this kind of checking, too, in a document that has words like VisiCorp and MEGAbux. By the way, WordPerfect 6.0's Speller finally recognizes WordPerfect with that capitalized *P* in the middle!

### Add Irregularly Capitalized Words to the Supplemental Dictionary

If there are company names or brand names that you type, such as Visi-Corp or MEGAbux, which use odd capitalization, choose Add when you're queried on them to add them to the supplemental dictionary.

### Switch Supplemental Dictionaries during a Spell Check

Halfway through the document, you come across a big section with medical terminology and you want to switch to your medical supplemental dictionary! No problem. Just choose Supplemental Dictionary from the Speller's Dictionaries menu when the Speller can't find a word. Highlight the name of the supplemental dictionary you want to switch to and choose OK.

### WordPerfect Can Keep a Dictionary for One Document

Choose Document Dictionary from the Add To pop-up list when the Speller asks you about a word, and that word will be stored in the document's dictionary, not in the supplemental dictionary. This is handy for special words that you know you won't be using anywhere else, because it helps keep your supplemental dictionary small, which speeds up spell-checking.

### Stop Spell-Checking and Resume It Later

If you're spell-checking a really big document, you may want to take a break. But you're not through, and the document hasn't been saved yet! It's OK. Exit from the Speller; then save the document. When you come back, start the Speller and choose **T**o End of Document from the **C**heck menu. WordPerfect will check from the point where you left off (assuming the cursor is still there) to the end of the document.

If you've exited WordPerfect, you can find the spot where you left off quickly by pressing **Ctrl+Q** when you retrieve that document again, if you've set up your preferences to have WordPerfect set that QuickMark (see Chapter 4) or if you've remembered to press **Ctrl+Shift+Q** to set a QuickMark yourself.

### Combine WordPerfect Versions 5.1 and 6.0 Supplemental Dictionaries

Your supplemental dictionary is in many ways more important than your main dictionary, because it contains all the words you add when you spell-check documents. If you've been using WordPerfect 5.1, you probably have a nice, big supplemental dictionary (mine was over 500 words) that you don't want to have to create over again by choosing Add every time the Speller runs across one of those terms. Instead, use this slick trick to get all the words you added to the dictionary in Word-Perfect 5.1 into the WordPerfect 6.0 supplemental dictionary.

Since the WordPerfect 5.1 supplemental dictionary is simply a document, open it in WordPerfect 6.0. Now—the slick trick: Run the Speller on it. Add all the words that it queries you about to your WordPerfect 6.0 dictionary by choosing Add every time the Speller stops at a word.

That's it; now you've got all your previously added words in the version 6.0 supplemental dictionary.

### Getting a Word Count

Look as you might, you can't find Word Count on any Speller menu like it used to be. Here's how to get a word count.

Choose Document Info from the File menu. The program will gather statistics about your document. When it's done, you'll see a dialog box showing all sorts of information about your document.

To get a word count of a section of a document, mark it as a block first and then choose Document Info.

---

## Numbers Don't Count in Word Counts

In a word count, numbers aren't counted as words unless they have a hyphen in them, like phone numbers. The date October 28, 1951 is considered one word. This is a little quirk you may not be aware of.

---

### Put Replacement Words in the Dictionary

If there's a word you want to use as a replacement word, put it in the dictionary. Or add a word as an alternate word. Isn't it maddening when WordPerfect doesn't recognize a word like Macintosh (the computer) and insists that it's Mackintosh (the jacket)? Put words like these in your supplemental dictionary and the program will suggest them as alternates when you type things like Macintosh.

Also, I seem to be incapable of typing the word *document* in any other way than *dcuement,* but WordPerfect insists that it can't make sense of this or suggest a replacement. If there are words that you habitually mistype like this, add them to the supplemental dictionary along with the correct replacement. Here's how to do it:

1. Start the Speller and click Add.

2. Type the word, such as Macintosh. Choose Replacement to have WordPerfect correct your typical mistakes, such as typing *dcuement* for document (Figure 7.11). Click Insert to put it in the list. Choose Alternatives to tell the Speller to list a new

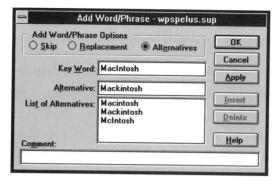

**Figure 7.11** Adding words to the supplemental dictionary

word as a suggestion for a misspelled word. Click Apply to update the supplemental dictionary with the new words.

### Put Replacements for Acronyms in the Dictionary

Here's another slick trick you'll appreciate if you have to type a lot of long, complex names like Multiphasic Industries, Inc., or Chief Operating Officer. Put those phrases in as replacements so that you can type *MII* or *COO* in your document. If you've selected **A**uto Replace from the Speller's **O**ptions menu, your replacement words will automatically be replaced when you run the Speller on the document.

You can do the same thing with WordPerfect's search and replace or abbreviations features, but putting the replacement in the dictionary assures that each occurrence gets caught (or, at least, brought to your attention) when you run the Speller.

### Turn Off the Speller in Part of the Document

If there's part of a document that you don't want to have spell-checked because it contains proper names, street addresses, or technical terms that the Speller doesn't know about, just disable the Speller for that part of the document.

Select the text that you don't want the Speller to check. Then choose **L**anguage from the **T**ools menu and check Disable Writing Tools.

### Find the Right Word to Use with the Thesaurus

Put the cursor on the word you want to find a substitute for and then choose **T**hesaurus from the **T**ools menu, or press **Alt+F1**. If WordPerfect has alternate words in its dictionaries, it will suggest them. If you see one you like, click on it and choose Replace.

### Double-Click on a Word to Look Up Related Words

If you don't like any of the words the Thesaurus is showing you, try this handy tip. Double-click on any word with a dot next to it that seems to be close to what you're looking for. The dot indicates that more words can be looked up for a word. You'll see a list of related words.

You can type a word in the Word box and choose Look Up if you want to look up a word that's not being displayed.

### If the Cursor Isn't on a Word...

No problem. If the cursor is between two words, the Thesaurus looks up the word that's to the *left* of the cursor.

### Use the History Command in the Thesaurus

Click on History to see a list of words that you've already looked up. If you saw a "good" word a couple of steps previously and now think that you want to use it, use this History command to trace the path you followed through the Thesaurus.

### Review Your Document before You Move On

Although the Thesaurus is "smart" enough to match the capitalization of the word it replaces in your document, look closely to make sure it matches the context of the surrounding words. A verb may need a different tense, for example, or you may need to add endings such as "s" and "es" for plurals or "ing" and "ed." For example, if you highlighted "indexing," the Thesaurus shows choices for "index."

### Run the Speller before You Run Grammatik

You'll speed up the process of checking your document if you run the Speller before using Grammatik, because it won't ask you about spelling mistakes. Turn off spell-checking in Grammatik by unchecking the Rule Class box when a spelling error is brought to your attention.

### Turn Off Features You Don't Want Grammatik to Check

Grammatik will automatically check for all kinds of things, such as spelling errors, periods inside words, and so forth, unless you tell it not to. You can speed up Grammatik by turning off some of these options. Also, if you write documents that contain a lot of things like DOS filenames, such as FEB.WK3 or MARCH.DOC, you may want Grammatik to ignore periods within words. Choose **C**hecking Options from Grammatik's **O**ptions menu to see what you can turn off.

### Get Help about What Grammatik's Doing

Grammatik has its own help system. If Grammatik really throws you with some of its rules, click on any underlined phrase to get help on what it's about.

### Leave Off Checking in Grammatik and Set a Bookmark

Checking a long document can get tedious. If you want to stop before you've finished, close the Grammatik window and set a bookmark (press **Ctrl+Shift+Q**). Then, to resume later, locate your bookmark with **Ctrl+Q** and choose **T**o End of Document from Grammatik's Check menu.

---

## Grammatik's Standards May Not Be What You Think

You might think that the General writing style would be the most formal, but it's not. For the strictest interpretation of grammar and style, choose Business Letter, Report, Technical, or Proposal.

For a standard level of formality that lets you end sentences with prepositions and use "you" instead of suggesting "one," pick General, Memo, Documentation, Journalism, or Fiction. For the loosest interpretation, choose Fiction or Advertising. The Journalism style also lets you use colloquial language without querying you too often on it.

### Set Up Your Own Style in Grammatik

You can define a custom style for Grammatik to use. For example, you'll probably not want to use it for spell-checking, so set up a style that doesn't check spelling.

To set up your own style, choose **W**riting Style from the **O**ptions menu. Highlight a style that's closest to the one you want and click Edit. For example, you might pick General. You'll see a long list of things the program will check for (Figure 7.12). Uncheck the ones you don't want to use; then click Save and save your style as Custom 1, 2, or 3.

### Get Statistics about Documents without Running the Grammar Checker

If you don't want to check your grammar, you may still find Grammatik really useful for getting statistics about your document. It will give you a word count (more accurate than WordPerfect's), as well as a set of readability scores and many other things. To bypass the regular grammar checking, choose **St**atistics from Grammatik's **O**ptions menu when you start.

### Turn Off Grammatik in Part of your Document

This is a slick trick for marking sections of a document you've already checked, or for marking sections where you've done a bit of, shall we say, creative writing and you don't want the grammar checked. Just

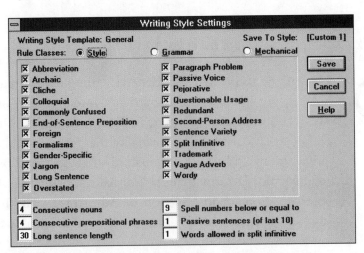

**Figure 7.12** Items the General style will check for

select the text you don't want checked and choose **L**anguage from the **T**ools menu. Check Disable Writing Tools.

# Twenty-First Century Tricks

Although the 21st century isn't quite here yet, WordPerfect lets you do some pretty amazing things. For example, it lets you create *interactive documents*—ones in which you can click to play a sound or hear a recorded message or display text that's in a completely different document. In fact, with the right software and hardware installed, Word-Perfect can even read your documents back to you—aloud. Many of these tricks are beyond the scope of this simple tricks book, but just in case you want to hear WordPerfect play sounds or speak to you, here are the tricks for how to do that.

First, you'll need a sound card and speakers installed in your system and working correctly. If you want to hear WordPerfect read aloud, you'll also need a text-to-speech synthesizer program such as Mono-logue (from First Byte, 800/556-6141).

### *Playing Sound in WordPerfect*

Windows comes with a few sound clips that you can include in your documents or just play for the fun of it. For the purposes of this trick, we'll assume that you're having fun—and amazing your office mates while you're at it.

Choose Sound from the Insert menu; then click the Insert button. In the File box (Figure 7.13), enter **C:\WINDOWS\TADA.WAV** (this is one of the sounds that Windows comes with, so it's undoubtedly on your system). Choose OK, and you'll see a speaker icon in your document in Page view (Figure 7.14). Double-click on it to hear the sound.

### *Making WordPerfect Read Aloud*

Highlight some text in your document. Now play the Readsel macro! (See the next section for shortcuts on how to play macros.)

Or, to have WordPerfect read a file, play the Readfile macro. These macros come with WordPerfect, but I bet you didn't know they were there.

**Figure 7.13** Inserting a sound clip

Remember, you need a program such as Monologue to make this trick work.

## Tricks for Using the Equation Editor

The equation editor in WordPerfect 6.0 is a very sophisticated tool for creating mathematical expressions. But you can also use it for some neat slick tricks, even if you aren't writing equations and using mathematical formulas. If you *are* creating equations, by all means use it, as

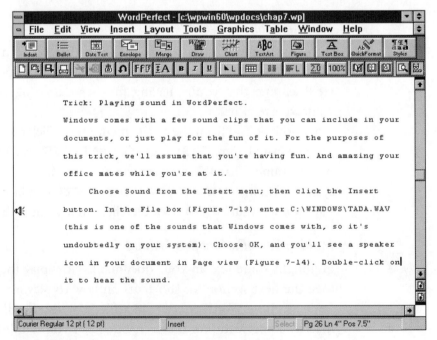

**Figure 7.14** The sound icon in the document

the equation editor will automatically follow its built-in rules so that your mathematical expressions look professional and polished. The only thing it *won't* do is solve your equations for you.

If you're a teacher, you may need to create math and algebra test questions, so I've included some relatively simple tricks here at first.

### Creating Simple Fractions

You may not think of simple fractions as equations, but to WordPerfect they are. (Actually, they're mathematical expressions, as "equation" implies an equality.) Instead of wrestling with learning all about the equation editor, just use this slick trick to create fractions: Choose **E**quation (or Inline Equation) from the **G**raphics menu. You'll be taken to the Equation Editor. Type x OVER y and press **Ctrl+F3**. Be sure to put the spaces around OVER (Figure 7.15). Click Close.

### A Times Sign in an Equation

You can use an asterisk (*) as a multiplication symbol, but those of you who teach elementary school probably prefer a times sign (x). To get one, use the WP Characters dialog box (**Ctrl+W**) and choose it from the Math/Scientific set, or use the TIMES command from the equation editor's palette. If you type an x in the equation editor, you'll get an italicized *x*.

### Choose a Different Font and Size for Equations

WordPerfect normally uses the same font and size as the rest of your document for equations, but it's often a nice touch to have them in a slightly smaller font (or larger, if there are very small symbols used) or a different font from the body text. Just click the Equation Font button on the Equation Editor button bar and pick a different font and size for that equation.

To change the font for *all* the equations in your document, the procedure's different. You'll need to change the equation box style. Click the Graphics Styles button (GraphicsSty) on the Graphics button bar; click Equation and choose Setup from the Options menu. Then choose Current Document and click OK. Click Edit; then click Settings and pick a different font and size.

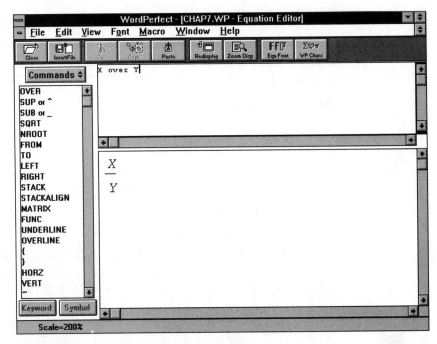

**Figure 7.15** Creating a simple fraction

### Creating an Inline Equation

WordPerfect normally displays an equation on a separate line. If you want a simple expression or fraction to be included on the same line as text, use this slick trick. It's not immediately obvious by any means: You have to add the Inline Equation option to your Graphics menu.

Choose **G**raphics Styles from the **G**raphics menu; then select Menu. Check Inline Equation; then click OK and Close. *Now* you can create an inline equation just like you create a regular displayed equation.

Don't try to create a complex, built-up equation as an inline equation. Do this only with simple equations that will fit on one line.

### Forcing Boldface, Italics, and Regular Text

The equation editor follows its own built-in set of rules about what to italicize. For example, it will automatically italicize Greek letters, as it assumes that they're variables. You can force the equation editor to do what you want it to if it's doing something different, though:

- To force italicized characters to be roman (regular) text, precede them with func and a space, as in func b to get a regular b.

- To force something to be in italics that isn't, precede it with ital and a space, as in ital {666}. You have to use curly braces around characters to group them together.

- To force something to be in boldface, precede it with bold and a space, as in bold {666}.

## Hard Returns on the Screen Don't Mean Line Breaks in Equations

You may think that an equation is correct on the screen as you create it in the equation editor, but hard returns that you get on the screen when you press **Enter** aren't interpreted as line breaks by the equation editor. To get equations to break on different lines, you'll have to use the pound sign (#) or the MATRIX, MATFORM, STACK, or STACKALIGN commands. For example, say that you want to create this set of equations, as shown:

$$c^3$$
$$c = d$$

To get the lines to break, enter the expressions as c^3# c = d.

### Spaces on the Screen Don't Mean Spaces in Equations

Use a tilde (~) to insert a space in an equation. Pressing the space bar doesn't insert a space in the equation editor, as you might think.

### Use the STACKALIGN Character to Specify an Alignment Character

Using the equation editor can get pretty sophisticated, so I'll shut up soon about all its fancy trimmings. But one last trick: Even if you don't create very elaborate equations, you may want to make them align on the equals sign when you're creating a test for your algebra class. You can hunt all night through the manual for how to do this. Here's the trick: Use the STACKALIGN command and the ampersand (&) to specify where you want lines in an equation to align. For example, typing stackalign {x &= y # bx + by &= cd} creates this set of equations:

$$x = y$$
$$bx + by = cd$$

There are *lots* more equation-editor tricks, but they're beyond the scope of this book.

# Simple Sorting Tricks

WordPerfect has some very sophisticated sorting abilities that are often used for sorting and merging records in mail-merge applications. But you can easily use those same sorting capabilities to do everyday things, such as alphabetizing a list of names or key words or sorting a list of addresses by zip code.

### *Alphabetizing a List*

Don't be afraid of WordPerfect's Sort feature. This simple trick shows you how easy it is to use to get a list into alphabetical order.

Let's assume you've got a list of vocabulary terms or key words like this one (but much longer, of course), with each entry on a separate line:

ROM

hard disk

mouse

floppy disk

RAM

keyboard

You want to make it alphabetical? Here's how.

**1** Select the list and press **Alt+F9**.

**2** If the dialog box you see looks like the one in Figure 7.16, which it will if you haven't sorted anything before, just press **Enter**. Your list will be alphabetized like this:

floppy disk

hard disk

keyboard

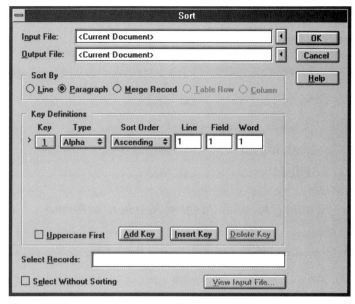

**Figure 7.16** The Sort dialog box

> mouse
>
> RAM
>
> ROM

If the Sort dialog box doesn't look like the one in Figure 7.16, make it look that one. The important thing is to have Key 1, Alpha, and Word 1 in the dialog box.

If your list is in a document all by itself, you don't have to select it first.

### *Alphabetizing by Last Name*

If you want to alphabetize names, though, you'll usually find that first names come before last names. If you use the preceding trick, the list will be sorted by first names, which probably isn't what you want. Say that you've got a list like this one:

| | |
|---|---|
| Rochelle Jackson | ext. 6723 |
| Willie Weston | ext. 9023 |
| Adele Harris | ext. 7823 |
| Mark Masters | ext. 7654 |

What you need to do is sort by last name, not by first name. The trick is to specify Word 2 as the key to sort on. Highlight the list (or cut and paste it into in a document of its own). Press **Alt+F9** and change Word to 2. Now click OK. That's all there is to it! Here's the alphabetized list:

| | |
|---|---|
| Adele Harris | ext. 7823 |
| Rochelle Jackson | ext. 6723 |
| Mark Masters | ext. 7654 |
| Willie Weston | ext. 9023 |

### Sorting Lists with Unequal Numbers of Items

This is a really "hard" one, but it's easy with a slick trick. Say that you have lists of names, but some folks have more names than others, like these:

Kay Yarborough Nelson

Henry Ford

Hillary Rodham Clinton

George Herbert Walker Bush

You want to sort it by last name, but if you specify Word 2 as the sort key, you won't get the list sorted right, because the last name is either Word 2, Word 3, or Word 4. Instead, use –1 as the word to sort on, and WordPerfect will sort by the last word in each line. Just enter –1 as the word number to sort on.

### What about "Jr." and Other Ends of Names?

You might think that a list with names like the following would pose an insurmountable problem to WordPerfect. Nope.

Arthur M. Schlesinger, Jr.

Cornelius Vanderbilt III

Werner von Braun

If you need to sort a list like this, separate the words that you want the program to treat as one word with a hard space (**Ctrl+space bar**) instead of simply pressing the space bar. For example, in this list you'd separate Schlesinger and Jr., Vanderbilt and II, and von and Braun with a hard space and then sort on word –1.

---

### If a List Has Tabs, It Has Fields

In WordPerfect, a *field* is text that's separated by tabs. If a list isn't getting sorted as you want, check to see if there are tabs in it. The text after the first tab is Field 2, for example.

---

### Sorting Addresses

To sort addresses—say, by zip code—separate each address with two hard returns so that the program thinks each address is a paragraph. Or separate them with hard page breaks, as in a list of addresses that are set up for mailing labels, for example. Use this same trick to sort bibliographic entries that have hard returns in them, too.

To sort paragraphs, when you see the Sort dialog box, click the Paragraph button.

# Mailing List Tricks

There's not much space in this tricks book to do justice to all WordPerfect's 6.0 features, but here are a couple of mail-merge tricks you can use.

### A Mailing List Can Be Used with Any Form Letter

I'll call a "form file" a "form letter" because that's the way most of us think about them. I'll also call a "data file" a "mailing list" for the same reason.

Once you've set up a mailing list, you can use it in any other form letter you set up. For example, you'd use the same mailing list for the form letter and for the mailing labels or envelopes you'd create to mail the letter in.

The trick is that *you don't have to use all the information in a mailing list*. Go ahead and create a good, general-purpose mailing list, including things like phone numbers and department numbers in it if you think you might need that information some day, as long as you have the original information handy as you're creating the list. Then just don't insert codes for those fields in your form letter and they won't get used. When you're ready to use that same mailing list for a name-and-address phone book, you'll have the information you need, organized and ready to use.

### Put Each Item to Be Used Independently into a Different Field

You'd probably think that a name such as "Dr. Benjamin S. Smith" should go into one name field, right? Wrong. If you put each item of information into a different field, you'll have lots more flexibility for using that mailing list with all sorts of documents—you know, the kind that say "Dear Dr. Smith" in one place and "Benjamin" in another. Put the person's title in one field, first name in another, middle initial in a third, last name in a fourth—you get the idea.

# Automatic Lists

WordPerfect can create automatic lists for you. This is a slick trick to use to have the program make lists of figure captions, tables, charts, equation numbers, and maps—including the page numbers they're on. You can use the same, basic slick trick to create keyword lists or lists of vocabulary words, as well. Tables of contents are simply a special type of list.

### You Don't Have to Mark Figure Captions for a List

WordPerfect automatically keeps track of figure captions for you. A "figure caption" is any caption given to a graphics box, whether it's a Text box, a Figure box, a Custom box, or an Equation box. Save yourself some time and don't bother setting up separate lists for captions of this sort, since the program does it for you.

## Watch Out for Page Numbering if You Use Reference Lists

 Your document's page numbering system can get mixed up if you include reference lists at the beginning of a document—say, just after the table of contents but before page 1. If you want the first text page of your document to stay page 1, go to that page and start page numbering from there.

### Duplicate Tables of Contents? You Defined It Twice.

Each time you define a table of contents, WordPerfect inserts a code in your document. It's easy to forget that you already defined a table of contents, because you don't see the actual table until you generate it. So, if you're getting two tables of contents, the reason is there are two [Def Mark:ToC] codes in your document. Open the Reveal Codes window, search for those codes, and delete one.

### Editing Tables of Contents Can Cause Trouble

If you manually edit a table of contents that WordPerfect has generated and then go back and generate the table of contents again, your changes will be lost. It's really easy to do this! And when you generate the document to create lists again, *all* your reference lists—indexes, figure captions, everything—are regenerated. Try not to edit tables of contents unless you know you're absolutely finished with the document. And even then, don't do it. Because you may retrieve that document two weeks from now and forget that you manually edited the table of contents . . . and there you'll be, in trouble all over again. Although, it's a pain if you need to delete a heading; add a new one or change wording; find the heading in the document and edit it; or mark or unmark it and then generate the table of contents again.

 ### Create Reference Lists after Documents Are Done

If you try to keep track of reference lists while you're writing a document, you'll go nuts. Go back after you're done and mark items for lists.

**The Mysteries of Generating**   When you "generate" a document (that's what WordPerfect calls it; don't blame me) by choosing Generate from the **T**ools menu or pressing **Ctrl+F9**, the program updates all the references in the document, including list items and their page numbers, cross references, footnotes, endnotes, indexes, tables of contents, and tables of authorities. Any of these items that you have in the document will change and be replaced with an updated version. If you've done any editing on them, *that editing will be lost.* Always edit the original item, not the list that's generated from it.

Also, be warned: If you generate lists, complete with page number references, and then go back and edit the document, the page numbers may change, throwing your list page numbers off. So, don't generate lists until you're pretty sure that you're through with a document. If you edit the document, generate the lists again.

## Slick Indexing Tricks

You probably won't have to create indexes very often, but if you do, there are a few slick tricks you can use to make things go faster.

### The Simplest Way to Index

The simplest way to create an index is to go through your document and create a *concordance file*, which is simply a list of all the terms, names, and phrases that you want to appear in the index. WordPerfect will use that concordance file to search your document and include any matching words, names, and phrases in the index it creates.

To create a concordance file, open a new document. Then type (or copy from the document you want to index) a list of the names, words, and phrases you want to have included in the index. End each entry with a hard return (press **Enter**). When you're done, save that document with a name that helps you remember it's a concordance file, such as CHAP8.CON.

Now define the index style on the page where you want the index to appear. Next to Filename under Concordance File, enter the name of the concordance file you created.

## A Concordance File Won't Give a Sophisticated Index

Unfortunately, a concordance file simply searches for the words and phrases that are in it and marks them as index entries. It can't tell that John Smith should be indexed as Smith, John, for example. It can't distinguish between plural and singular, either, so the word *computer* may get indexed while the words *computers* or *computing* won't, unless you've included all the variations in the concordance file. Also, if you don't give some thought to your index entries, you'll wind up with fairly meaningless items, like *budgets,* when what you really wanted to index was *annual budgets* and *quarterly budgets.* So the longer you spend setting up a concordance file, the more pleased you'll be with the results.

### Be Sure to Define a Page for Your Index

You won't get an index unless you define it and generate it, just like any other list. Indexes usually appear at the *end* of a document, so when you're ready to define the index, go to the end of the document; then press **Ctrl+Enter** to create a new page; finally, define your index there.

### Use Tables of Authorities for Bibliographies

Lots of folks think tables of authorities are used only in the legal profession as long, dull lists of precedents, statutes, and legislation. Not so. You can use WordPerfect's Tables of Authorities feature for any kind of bibliographic citation—as long as you know a few slick tricks.

Creating a table of authorities is like creating any other type of list in WordPerfect, except that you pick a format for each *section* of the table, and you can have as many as 16 different sections. Within each section, all the entries are alphabetized and the page numbers where the references fall are automatically inserted. Lawyers use the different sections for different types of legal citations—one section for statutes, another for precedents, and so on. If you're just creating a bibliography or a list of suggested readings, you'll need only one section, though.

---

### Delete the Code for the Index to Delete the Index

WordPerfect inserts a [Def Mark:Index] code when you define an index. If you decide that you don't want the index, locate and delete the code. Otherwise, you'll get a new index every time you generate the document.

   Need it be said again that creating an index should be one of the last steps in document creation, after all the tables and graphics are in place and you've spell-checked the document and checked page breaks? Once you start editing a document again, page breaks will change, your index entries will be off, and you'll need to generate the document again. A great timewaster.

---

### Think About Your Table of Authority's Structure before Marking Citations

If you're going to create one of those complicated multisection tables of authorities, figure out what's going to go in which section *before you begin*. It will make life a lot easier if you've written down which section's supposed to include what type of reference.

## Slick Tricks for Footnotes and Endnotes

In case there's any confusion: Endnotes are notes that appear at the end of a document. Footnotes appear at the bottom of the page where the material they're referencing occurs. When to use which? This general rule works well, unless you have a teacher or professor telling you to do it another way (in which case, don't try to swim against the current): Use endnotes to cite sources, such as bibliographic references; use footnotes to expound on something that's mentioned in the text. You can have both footnotes and endnotes in a WordPerfect document. To keep things simple, both footnotes and endnotes are referred to simply as *notes* in these next slick tricks.

### Don't Type Note Text if It Exists in This or in Another Document

Don't forget that it's so easy to copy and paste in WordPerfect. If you're citing an author and a book title, with a publisher, place and year of publication, and so forth, don't type all that again if it's already in your document! Just copy and paste it into the note editing screen. Remember, you can copy from another document, too.

### Converting Footnotes to Endnotes

You've labored over a long paper, and then you find out that Professor Smith wants endnotes instead of footnotes. You could go back and search for each one and change it, but there's a slicker way. Play the Endfoot macro that comes with WordPerfect.

Likewise, there's a Footend macro that converts footnotes to endnotes if you need to do that.

---

### You Can't Have Footnotes in a Table Header Row

You can have footnotes in tables, but if you try to put one in a table header row (a header that you want to be repeated if the table breaks across two pages), WordPerfect will change it to an endnote. Be aware of this.

---

### Easily Moving Notes from One Place to Another

You don't have to retype a note or re-create it in a different place. With WordPerfect 6.0, you can drag and drop notes to move them. Just select the note number and drag it to the new location.

Here's another way to move notes around easily. Open a Reveal Codes window, put the cursor on the [Note Num] code, and press **Ctrl+X** to delete it. Move the cursor to a nw location and press **Ctrl+V** to paste it. You can copy notes this way with **Ctrl+C**, too. WordPerfect renumbers them correctly in their new locations.

Another slick way to copy a note is to delete it; then Undo it (**Ctrl+Z**) in the same location; then move to a new location and un-delete it (press **Esc**).

### Don't Use Numbers for Footnotes in a Table Full of Numbers

It will help your readers a lot if you change the footnote numbering system to letters (or symbols; see the next trick) instead of numbers in tables of numbers. They'll be able to tell which is a note and which is the body of the table.

   When you're done with the table, you can go back to using numbers for footnotes in the body of the text.

### Using WordPerfect Characters As Symbols for Notes

Want to use a system of daggers, double daggers, and so forth as your note numbering system? Try this slick trick. Choose **F**ootnote from the **I**nsert menu; then choose **O**ptions. In the dialog box that you'll see, choose Characters as the numbering method. In the Characters text box, press **Ctrl+W** and choose a special WordPerfect character. Use the Typographic Symbols set to choose some very interesting symbols, such as section symbols, daggers, and so forth.

### Changing the Note Number

You can force WordPerfect to use a specific number for a note. This is a slick trick to know if you're building a large document from smaller ones, but not using WordPerfect's Master Document feature. Choose **F**ootnote or **E**ndnote from the **I**nsert menu; then pick **N**ew Number and type the number you want in the dialog box you'll see.

### Restoring a Note Number

This happens all too often: You're editing a note's text in the note editing screen, and you make a mistake and delete the note number! You've deleted the note, and simply typing the number won't get it back. Press **Ctrl+Z** or **Ctrl+Shift+Z** to undelete it.

### Keeping Footnotes Together

Doesn't it drive you crazy when WordPerfect splits a footnote onto two pages when you want to keep it on one page? It will normally keep only half an inch of text on the page before splitting the note between two pages. Here's how to force the program to keep footnotes intact if there's room on the page. First, go to the beginning of your document!

**1** Choose **F**ootnote from the **I**nsert menu; then choose **O**ptions.

**2** Choose **A**mount of Footnote to Keep Together and type a measurement. WordPerfect will interpret what you enter as inches unless you've changed the default units of measure the program uses. So if your longest footnote is 2 inches, enter **2**.

For a fancy touch, check the Insert Continued Message box so that if you wind up with any footnotes that are longer than two inches, or whatever you entered, the program will print "(continued)" with the note so that the reader will look on the next page for the rest of it.

---

### Check Page Breaks When Using Footnotes

By all means, do a quick run-through in Page view before you print documents that have footnotes in them, especially if your document is going to be bound and you want facing pages to balance each other by being of equal length. Normally, if the page isn't filled with text, WordPerfect puts the footnote after the last line of text instead of at the bottom of the page. But in the Footnote Options dialog box, there's a check box for Place Notes at Bottom of Page. On a page that has two lines of text and one footnote, you'll get lots of white space by having Place Notes at Bottom of Page checked. But your pages will balance if that's what you want.

---

### Setting Up Indents in Notes

WordPerfect's default style is to use a plain tab after the note number, which means that the second line of the note will wrap back to the left margin instead of being neatly indented. This is what it will look like:

1. Nelson, Kay Yarborough. *Friendly WordPerfect for Windows.* (New York: Random House, 1992).

You may prefer a block-indented style in which the second line aligns with the first, like this:

1. Nelson, Kay Yarborough. *Friendly WordPerfect for Windows.* (New York: Random House, 1992).

To get this type of indentation in your notes, just press **F7** before you start to type the text of the note.

### Changing the Note Style—And Font, Too

If you want the indented style shown in the preceding trick in *all* your notes, you'll need to edit the footnote (or endnote) style.

Choose **F**ootnote and then **O**ptions from the Insert menu; then choose In Note under Edit Numbering Style. Press **End** to move to the end of the codes. Then press **F7** to create the indent in the style.

You may also need to set a tab for the indent if the indentation is more than you want.

### Changing the Note Font

While you're editing the footnote style, why not change the font as well? It's a nice touch to have footnotes and endnotes in a slightly smaller font than the rest of your document. You may even want to pick a completely different font for notes. Press **Ctrl+F** to open the Font dialog box while you're editing a note style. Put the font-change code at the beginning of the note (press **Home**) so that the note number will be in that font.

### Changing the Note Style in Text

Choose In Text in the Footnote Options dialog box to change the font and size for the actual note number that appears in the body of the document. This is also how you can change the note numbering system from superscript to regular numbers, maybe boldface or something, either because you don't like the way your printer handles them or because you're preparing an article for a magazine that doesn't want you to use superscripts. Delete the [Suprscpt On] code and then insert the codes for whatever format you want footnote numbers in text to have around the [Footnote Num Display] code, such as putting parentheses around the number or using [Bold].

### WordPerfect Automatically Spell-Checks Notes

You don't have to go through your notes one by one, checking the spelling of each one, or use any other fancy technique to get the program to spell-check text in notes. Don't worry; WordPerfect checks notes when you spell-check a document.

### Search for the Note You're Looking For

Instead of going through your notes one by one, use the Search feature to locate the specific note you're looking for, with very little fuss. Just press **F2** and then choose **C**odes from the **M**atch menu. Type footn or endn and press **Enter**, depending on what you're hunting, to go straight to either of these in the list. Now, click Find Next or Find Previous in the Find dialog box. If the first note found isn't the one you want, click Find Next or Find Previous to go to the next one, or close the Find dialog box to get it out of your way and then use the shortcut **Shift**+**F2** to find the next occurrence or **Alt**+**F2** to find the previous occurrence.

This trick works fine if you're familiar with which note number is for what, or if you can tell from the context of the document. To check the actual text of the note, keep the Reveal Codes window open while you search.

---

## Turning Off Line Numbering Isn't the Same As Removing *It*

You turn on line numbering by choosing **L**ine Numbering from the **L**ayout menu. You use the same dialog box to turn it off by unchecking the Turn Line Numbering On box. But to actually *remove* line numbers from your document, open a Reveal Codes window and delete the [Ln Num:On] code that's creating the line numbers. You can search for it by pressing **F2**, then choosing **C**odes from the **M**atch menu, and searching for the Ln Num code.

---

### Search for Words and Phrases in Notes

Say that you don't recall whether you want to edit note 33 or 39, but you do remember that the note you want to edit has the name *William Shakespeare* in it. Press **F2** and enter William Shakespeare as the text to find. Then choose Include Headers, Footers, etc. in Find from the **O**ptions menu in the Find dialog box. Now WordPerfect will search through the text of notes as well as the body of the document.

### Comparing Documents

If you need to check the differences between a revised version of a document (the one on the screen) and a version of the document that you've saved already, use WordPerfect's Compare Document feature. This is a very useful feature if you have to work with contracts, because you can see quickly what's changed.

You can get really confused, though, by what's new, what's been moved, what's been deleted, and so forth in two versions of the same document. Plus, if the power goes out, any changes you've made to the document that's on the screen (but haven't saved) will be lost. Save your document under a name that's different from the one you saved it as already (use the Save As command). Then compare the two saved documents. Here's how to do it.

First, save the document on the screen under another name if the document you're comparing it to (another version) has the same name. From the File menu, choose Compare Document and then choose Add Markings. Pick which method you want WordPerfect to use when comparing the documents (tip: choosing by Word, the default, is the slowest but the most accurate).

WordPerfect will compare the documents, using redlining and strikeout. The text that's in the saved document that *isn't* in the document on the screen is struck out, and the text that's in the document on the screen but *isn't* in the saved version is redlined.

### Keeping That Struck-Out Text

If you want to retain the struck-out text in the compared document, use this trick. To strip out all the [Stkout On] codes in the document: Press **Ctrl+F2**, choose Codes from the Match menu, search for the StkOut codes, and replace them with nothing. Make sure that Include Headers, Footers, etc. in Find is selected on the Options menu, and all those Strikeout codes will be deleted from your document, as well as from any footnotes and endnotes in it.

---

### Don't Save the Compared Document

Not unless you want a document with all that redlining and strikeout, that is. If you should happen to save it by mistake, you can remove the redlining and strikeout. But be aware that the struck-out *text* will be removed as well, not just the strikeout markings.

To remove the markings and struck-out text, choose Compa**re** Document from the **F**ile menu; then choose **R**emove Markings. Pick Remove Strikeout Text Only or Remove Markings and Strikeout Text and choose OK. Either way, you lose the struck-out text.

If you do this and go, "Oh, no!" press **Ctrl+Z** for that handy Undo feature. Right now.

---

# Paragraph Numbering and Outlining Tricks

With WordPerfect, it's easy to create numbered paragraphs that will automatically change as you add or delete more numbered paragraphs. This is ideal if you have to create multiple-choice test questions, or in any situation where you want numbered paragraphs, such as numbered headings in a technical document. You can use the same technique to create bulleted lists without having to do much thinking about the special characters involved.

### Instant Lists

You saw this trick back in Chapter 3, but here it is again. To create a bulleted or numbered list instantly (almost), type the text you want to have in the list, pressing **Enter** after each item. Then select the text and click the Bullet button on the WordPerfect button bar. Pick the style you want and click OK.

Now, here are some tricks for this feature:

♦ If you're typing a list, you probably want to have a new number or bullet appear whenever you press **Enter**, at least until you get through with the list. In the Bullets & Numbers dialog box, check New Bullet or Number on ENTER.

♦ If you don't want a new number or bullet to appear each time you press **Enter**—either because you want to be able to insert some blank lines in your list or because it's just a short list— leave that box blank. Instead, press **Ctrl+Shift+B** to insert a new bullet or number.

♦ If you've typed a list and later decide that an item or two in it shouldn't be numbered or bulleted, select it. Then click the Bullet button again and choose <None>. This will turn off the number or bullet for the paragraph you've selected.

### Quickly Creating an Outline

Right-click in the left margin of your text to open a QuickMenu. Choose Outline; then pick the style you want to use, check the Start New Outline box, and press **Enter** or click OK.

### Better Display the Outline Feature Bar, Too

The previous trick will let you create a plain-vanilla, short outline easily. But if you're going to use collapsible outlining, create long outlines, or do heavy-duty editing in outlines, display the Outline feature bar by choosing Outline from the Tools menu.

### Alt+Shift+T Converts Text to an Outline Item (or Vice Versa)

When you're creating an outline with the Outline feature bar displayed, special level markers will be displayed to the left of your text. T stands for regular text, and the numbers that you see represent the level number in the outline. To convert an outline item to regular text, just select it and press **Alt+Shift+T**, without bothering to turn outlining off and then on again.

### Stop Creating an Outline with Alt+Shift+C

To remove the outline feature bar from your screen and thereby turn off outline mode, just press **Alt+Shift+C**.

### Inserting an Unnumbered Line in an Outline

Every time you press **Enter** when Outline is on, you get a new number. To create an unnumbered, blank line when the outline feature bar is being displayed, press **Alt+Shift+T** and then press **Enter**. Press **Alt+Shift+T** again to switch back to outlining.

### Inserting a Tab in an Outline

Normally, pressing **Tab** in an outline decreases the outline item one level. To move to a real tab stop, press **Ctrl+Tab** or **F7** (Indent).

### Type the Text of Outlines First

You'll find that it's a lot more efficient to type the text of an outline all at the same level (by just pressing **Enter** after each paragraph) and then turn on WordPerfect's Outline feature and indent the paragraphs to the levels you want. Go back and put the cursor on the outline number of each paragraph and then press **Tab** or **Shift+Tab** until it's at the appropriate level.

### Drag and Drop to Edit Outline Entries, Too

You can drag and drop to move text around in an outline.

**Ctrl+Z** (Undo) will put a moved outline entry back where it came from after you've moved it to the wrong place. This saves you figuring out where it came from originally, which can be very confusing in a long, complicated outline.

### Select an Outline Entry by Clicking on Its Symbol

Click on the nonprinting symbol in the left margin to quickly select an outline entry, without having to figure out exactly what to select on the screen.

### Use Outline Entries As Headings in a Document

If you need numbered headings in a document, create them as outline entries. Then, if you add or delete a heading, WordPerfect will automatically update the numbers in the other headings and subheadings so that you don't have to do it.

Also, if you use outline entries as headings, it's easy to look at the structure of your document at a glance by picking which level numbers you want to show.

# What Next?

. . . . . . . . . . . . . . . . . . . . . . . . . . . . . . . . . . . .

Exploring the program's extensive Help system on your own is an excellent way to start down the path of mastering the more technical and sophisticated aspects of WordPerfect.

The eclectic collection of tricks in this book may have sharpened your appetite for mastering more advanced skills in WordPerfect 6.0. Gordon McComb's *WordPerfect 6.0 Power Tools* (New York, Random House, 1993) is an excellent book that will take you farther along the path to mastering the more technical and sophisticated aspects of the program.

# Index

243